JOHN MAJOR
PRIME MINISTER

JOHN MAJOR
PRIME MINISTER

The PRESS ASSOCIATION

EDITED BY JOHN JENKIN
INTRODUCTION BY CHRIS MONCRIEFF

The PRESS ASSOCIATION

EDITED BY JOHN JENKIN
INTRODUCTION BY CHRIS MONCRIEFF

B L O O M S B U R Y

First published in Great Britain 1990
Bloomsbury Publishing Limited, 2 Soho Square, London W1V 5DE

The publishers would like to thank the following, without whose active co-operation this book could not have been produced: Roger Pring, Isobel Jacobs, Craig Cornock, Rachel King, Tom Fraser, Bridget Coaker (picture research), Ben Preston, PA News Library, PA Photo Library, PA Darkroom, *Cambridge Evening News* (Robert Satchwell, Editor, Cedric Tarrant, Picture Editor, and Peter Wells, News Editor), PA Editorial (Frank Vincini and Bob Gales) and PA Graphics.

Also, our thanks go to journalists of the *Cambridge Evening News, Daily Express, Daily Mail, Daily Mirror, Daily Telegraph, Evening Standard, Financial Times, Guardian, Independent, London Gazette, Morning Star, Observer, People,* the Press Association, *Sunday Telegraph, Sunday Times* and *The Times.*

A CIP catalogue record for this book
is available from the British Library

ISBN 0-7475-0942-5

Printed and bound in Great Britain by Richard Clay plc, Bungay, Suffolk

CONTENTS

Introduction

By Chris Moncrieff, PA Political Editor

JOHN MAJOR, Mrs Thatcher's Crown Prince, is the very model of a self-made man.

The pencil-sharp politician, whose qualifications include being a former Chancellor of the Exchequer, Foreign Secretary, Chief Secretary to the treasury and son of a trapeze artist, once failed an arithmetic test that barred him from becoming a bus conductor.

Famous as the only Cabinet Minister who has been on the dole, the 47-year-old Londoner finds himself in the highest office in the land five years before he planned to be ready.

Now a durable whizz-kid after eight government jobs in as many years, Mr Major is grey haired, generally grey suited and has six identical grey ties.

What is even more splendid is that John Major has displayed his revulsion at the very idea that anyone should try to transform him into something that he is not..

He said: "I am what I am and people will have to take me for what I am. The image-makers will not find me in their tutelage."

If his voice has become more rounded, he patiently explained to an excited reporter soon after his accession, it was because he was suffering from a cold. No, he had not changed the length of his hair, the style of his suits, or the colour of his shirts. Moreover, he was perfectly content to remain "the same plug-ugly as I always was on television".

This certainly is a man of sheer ability, without a devious thought in his head, to whom conspiracies and underhand dealings are unknown, who has surged relentlessly to the top without apparently making any effort whatsoever.

That in itself is astonishing in the House of Commons which is constantly seething with rumour, intrigue, character assassination and worse. Only a few months before he was elected, John Major was such an unsuspected candidate that his name was never even mentioned by the shadowy traders in tittle-tattle who chatter in the dark corners of the Palace of Westminster.

Indeed, what price would anyone have offered for the prospects of a former building-site labourer becoming leader of the Conservative and Unionist Party, never mind Chancellor of the Exchequer? Even at a time when Conservative politicians were having to apologise for being Old Etonians and the man-of-the-people grammar school-reared individual was to become the party archetype, John Major had an unlikely, even bizarre, upbringing for the post of Tory Prime Minister.

His father Tom was what he described as a sort of

peripatetic circus artist, who in later life owned a farm in Shropshire and then developed a business in moulding garden gnomes.

John himself was born in 1943 in the relatively prosperous Worcester Park commuter suburb. But when his father's business collapsed, the family was forced to move severely down-market to a flat on the top of a large, rambling, somewhat ramshackle house in Brixton.

For his family, this was a come-down in the world. For John it was near-rapturous, for it was within walking distance of the Oval cricket ground, where he developed his love for the game.

John Major remains proud of the way his parents made sacrifices on his behalf. "Any difficulties from that time were shielded from me as much as it is possible to do so, both by my father, who was pretty bedridden, and by my mother," he said.

He was not an ideal schoolboy, and had a far from complimentary view about the people who ran Rutlish Grammar School, Wimbledon when he was a pupil there. But the feeling was mutual.

John was described in one school report as too cheeky, a view which it is hard to reconcile now with the self-effacing, modest man who occupies 10 Downing Street.

For his part he says he did not like the regimentation of school. "I did not like the unthinking obedience that people wanted. I didn't always agree with decisions and didn't see why I shouldn't say so.

"I often did say so. I just felt generally disgruntled and no doubt was generally very disgruntling."

John left school at 16, something he does not now care to dwell on. And in one radio interview he responded testily to questions about his schooling and his supposed paucity of academic qualifications.

When the interviewer had the temerity to suggest that he had secured only two school certificates, John Major retorted: "That is rubbish. I am not going to put the record straight. It has nothing to do with anybody else."

It was actually his own decision to leave school at 16, to go out and earn some money and to make life easier for his hard-pressed parents. But he takes a philosophical view of that, saying that he learned a great deal more by not being at school than he would have done had he stayed.

He plunged into the grown-up world in an ill-fitting suit as a trainee accountant with Price Forbes in the City of London. That, however, plainly did not appeal to the lad, so he discarded the uncomfortable attire and entered the casual market, labouring, mixing cement and doing things like that which in later years he was to describe as extremely educational.

For a period of two years he did a routine and dull job at the Electricity Board, in the Elephant and Castle, South London. But the tedium was compensated for by the great host of rich characters by whom he was surrounded.

This period was punctuated by spells on the dole, when he received £2.87 a week unemployment pay. "I used to go job-hunting in the morning and when that came to naught, as it did come to naught, I trotted off to the pictures for a shilling in the afternoon."

But eventually this type of life palled and John Major decided to return to the City to banking. But he became bored with the sedentary life. He wanted to travel. At that stage, in the mid-1960s, he had not merely never been abroad but the furthest he had ever travelled was to Southend and back on his bicycle.

So he moved from the District Bank to the Standard Chartered Bank, where the prospects of an overseas posting were greater. And as the Biafran War was raging at the time and as to use his own modest words he was more disposable than most, off he went to Nigeria.

It was here that his left leg was smashed up in a road accident. He returned to Britain and spent the best part of a year in a National Health Service hospital having it put to rights.

But even now, if he walks too far, his knee (he lost his knee-cap in the smash) swells up like a balloon.

It is probably on account of this that the Labour Party, highly suspicious of Mrs Thatcher's attitude towards the National Health Service, actually believe John Major when he says, by inference, that the NHS is safe in his hands.

But behind this unconventional background there lurked in the man's mind a hankering after a political life. That desire was by no means lessened when his career at the Standard Bank brought him into close contact with the chairman, Lord Barber, who as Anthony Barber had been Mr Edward Heath's Chancellor of the Exchequer.

This business acquaintanceship brought him a visit to the International Monetary Fund meeting in 1976, only three years before he was to become a Member of Parliament. But by an odd contrast, the man who had earlier encouraged him in what what was later to become an ambition to enter politics was not Lord Barber but Colonel Marcus Lipton, his local Labour MP, and one of the most active, if venerable, MPs in the Commons at the time.

The Colonel had taken him on a tour of the House of Commons, but his influence on the lad plainly had little effect. For the young John's persuasion led him to the Conservative Party rather than to Labour, although he readily acknowledged then, as he does now, that Labour operated with very benevolent intentions in his home district of Brixton.

John got himself elected to Lambeth Borough Council and as chairman of the local housing committee he won praise from some strange quarters.

A fellow member, Mr Ken Livingstone (who became leader of the former Greater London Council and then

Labour MP for Brent East), said about him: "John Major would get up and say that we had to help people. Many of us on the left were acutely embarrassed about the previous record of Labour."

It was around this time, in 1970, that John met his demure wife Norma, who was not built for public life but who accepts it with grace and cheerfulness. The couple met when he was campaigning in the Greater London Council elections of that year.

He recalls: "It took us all of three weeks to get engaged. But it did take us six months before we were married." It was after the marriage, the honeymoon and the settling down that John Major started to hunt around for a parliamentary seat. They have two children.

John fought the hopeless seat of St Pancras in both the February and the October elections of 1974. Then he did what anyone else would do having been blooded in a Labour stronghold: sought a seat which gave him a realistic chance of being returned to Westminster as a Conservative MP.

He made a bee-line for Huntingdon, his hopes not high but his spirit in good trim. To his utter astonishment he made it to the last four even though, as he admits, "Nobody knew who I was." And then, to his even further amazement, he won through to become the candidate.

John Major has never sat on the Opposition benches. Indeed, he has sat behind only one Prime Minister. The day that she stepped into Downing Street in May, 1979, reciting St Francis of Assisi, he was the new boy at the House of Commons.

Who at that time could have considered that this gangling figure, untrammelled by social graces, swearing the oath of allegience in halting and unimpressive tones, might be Britain's next Prime Minister? It was unthinkable.

And even his steady but unspectacular upward progress did not attract, until only weeks before it happened, any kind of speculation that he was heading for 10 Downing Street.

Indeed, Norman Tebbit's tip that Major might be a future contender for the leadership was regarded in 1987 as mildly eccentric.

Major was as surprised as his colleagues suddenly to find himself impeccably positioned to fill the vacancy so unexpectedly created by Mrs Thatcher in November, 1990.

Two years after his arrival at Westminster, Mr Major became parliamentary private secretary to a series of Home Office Ministers. This is a job akin to being a batman to an officer in the army. A PPS is little more than a minister's bag-carrier and general factotum.

But it is a rash MP who sneers at such a job. For it is a first sign that someone has noticed you. And the next step is invariably a junior minister's post.

Between 1983 and 1985 he was a Government Whip, before becoming a junior and then a middle-ranking Social

John Major and his wife, Norma, in the garden of their Canbridgeshire home.

Security Minister. It was here that when he appeared reluctant to authorise cold-weather payments to old people, he altered the system and found the money to do it.

As he continued to rise, he observed with his customary modesty: "I guess I have been lucky in that I have been in the right place at the right time, without which you don't have good fortune in politics."

That may be modest but it is true as well. There are now people in the Labour Party who, if they had been at Westminster in a different era, would have been Cabinet Ministers. But now, with 11 years in Opposition, they have been right through the age when they could be considered for high ministerial office. They will never make it even if Labour succeed at the next election.

It was immediately after the 1987 general election that Mrs Thatcher found a place for him in her Cabinet as Chief Secretary to the Treasury. That is one of the key but least spectacular of all the senior ministerial posts.

As such, you are expected to play very much the second fiddle to the Chancellor, but at the same time do most of the unglamorous grind, the work that keeps the Government going, but rarely puts the operative in the limelight.

It was his skill and persuasion (a CBI man once said of him, "He has the most courteous way of saying no") in restricting the budgets of the big Government spending departments that endeared him more than anything else to Margaret Thatcher.

So when, in her highly controversial Cabinet reshuffle of July, 1989, she abruptly removed Sir Geoffrey Howe from the Foreign Office, she had no hesitation in putting John Major in his place. You could see him blinking with surprise as he stepped into the Foreign Office that first bright July morning.

When he telephoned his wife to say he had been made Foreign Secretary, she simply did not believe him. "You are winding me up," she insisted.

But when it dawned on her that her husband was being serious she said she felt "physically sick".

John Major was not to be at the Foreign Office for long, but long enough to take part in a Commonwealth Heads of Government meeting at Kuala Lumpur later that year, when the issue of South African sanctions was the dominant issue.

This was the time when he was unfairly tagged with the label "Mrs Thatcher's poodle". They appeared to issue conflicting reports of events, reports which later became harmonious. "What happened," he explained, "was that we offended the amour propre of the diplomatic corps ... The next morning I was astonished to read that there had been a huge row between the Prime Minister and me." His short-lived presence in the Foreign Office attracted a gale of fresh air into that musty building. His influence remained there long after he had departed.

But soon the signs that Mrs Thatcher had marked him out as her favourite to succeed him – although not as quickly as it was to happen – came with the sudden and surprising resignation in October, 1989, of the then Chancellor, Nigel Lawson.

Almost within minutes of Mr Lawson breaking the news – he beat Downing Street to it – the then Prime Minister announced that Mr Major would take his place.

At the Treasury he tackled the battle against inflation with vigour. He said: "Inflation is poison to investment, poison to competitiveness, and poison to industrial relations. And inflation is social poison – it punishes the saver, the pensioner, the weakest in our society." He remained at the Treasury for the last traumatic 12 months of Mrs Thatcher's "reign", when event after event gradually destabilised her until she was forced to resign on November 22, 1990.

John Major was loyal to the last. He seconded her nomination in the first ballot in the leadership contest when she failed to win outright. He was poised to sign her nomination papers for the second ballot – he was recovering at home in Cambridgeshire from a wisdom-tooth operation at the time – when she decided to quit.

He submitted his name for the second ballot and defeated his rivals, Michael Heseltine, the former Defence Secretary, and Foreign Secretary Douglas Hurd, falling just two votes short of outright victory.

The rules demanded that, even though the other two candidates were prepared to withdraw and pledged support for Major, there should be a third ballot with all three candidates taking part.

But Mr Cranley Onslow, chairman of the 1922 Committee of Tory back benchers which runs party elections, decreed that no third ballot was necessary.

So John Major, the classless man in the grey pinstripe suit, had made it. He was in No 10 Downing Street with the rest of the world still looking him up in Who's Who.

Listen to what others have said about him:

"Who is this nice man who has risen to the top without bloodletting, without revealing himself? Is he right, left or centre?" asked Le Figaro, the French daily newspaper.

"I like him and he is a very competent man, but I do not understand what he believes," commented Alan Beith, Liberal Democrats economics spokesman.

"He has a caring face. Not all women go for flamboyance," observed Gillian Shephard, Treasury Minister.

But he fits, more precisely than any other politician I know, the fine words in Hamlet: "There is nothing becomes a man as modest stillness and humility." John Major is all of that.

1

Member of Parliament

An unhappy and unsuccessful school career, a father who was bedridden and broke and a spell on the dole in the backstreets of Brixton were the unlikely elements that, combined with a security in the love of his family and an unshakable determination to win, provided the launching-pad for John Major's political career.

A Young Conservative at 16 and a Lambeth Councillor later, he had a secure job in banking and a happy and successful family life which in themselves might have been considered tribute enough to his steadfast, steely nature.

Charm, good manners, a remarkable memory and comprehension of figures and a talent for bringing others round to his point of view were all contributory factors in the rise and rise of the man who was to become Britain's youngest Prime Minister this century.

Tories' Choice

MR JOHN MAJOR, 33 year old international banker, of Beckenham, Kent, has been chosen as Parliamentary Conservative candidate for Huntingdonshire. The present Conservative MP, Sir David Renton, is retiring at the next election.

GENERAL ELECTION: Sir David Renton (C) 26,989; M.Dowson (Lab.) 17,745; D.Rowe (L.) 15,152. C. majority 9,244.

CAMBRIDGE EVENING NEWS

John Major was one of 250 candidates who put themselves forward for selection to fight the Huntingdonshire seat for the Tories. Once selected, he had to keep himself in the public eye for the three years between selection and the general election. This was one of ways that he did it.

Candidate attacks cut-back

Cambridgeshire's success in attracting new people could be its downfall if Whitehall does not come up with the cash to help cater for them, the Conservative prospective candidate for Huntingdonshire, Mr John Major, said.

Mr Major has attacked the Government cut-back in cash aid to Cambridgeshire and warned that if it continues Cambridgeshire could face severe problems.

"If we are not careful we will have the worst of possible results: more people flocking to Cambridgeshire and no jobs for them," he said. "We will be creating locally the problems of London at precisely the time the Government takes away the resources to deal with them."

"We must not let Cambridgeshire become a Cinderella county."

Mr Major said the Government cut in cash support to the county is grossly unfair and will lead to soaring rate bills combined with cuts in services. "This year the cut is £10 million notwithstanding an enormous population growth in the county that is leading to greater demands on education and the social services," he said.

"The unemployment situation, particularly for the young, is already acutely serious, especially in Huntingdon and Peterborough."

Mr Major said the situation in Huntingdon is grim. At least six youngsters are chasing each vacancy and Huntingdon shows the most serious rate of deteriorating opportunities in the county.

"Over the past two years, whilst the number of available and suitable jobs has remained steady, the number of the unemployed has multiplied ten-fold," he said.

"These facts show the problems of growth that Cambridgeshire faces and they also emphasise the great difficulties there will be if the rate support grant cuts are not restored."

CAMBRIDGE EVENING NEWS

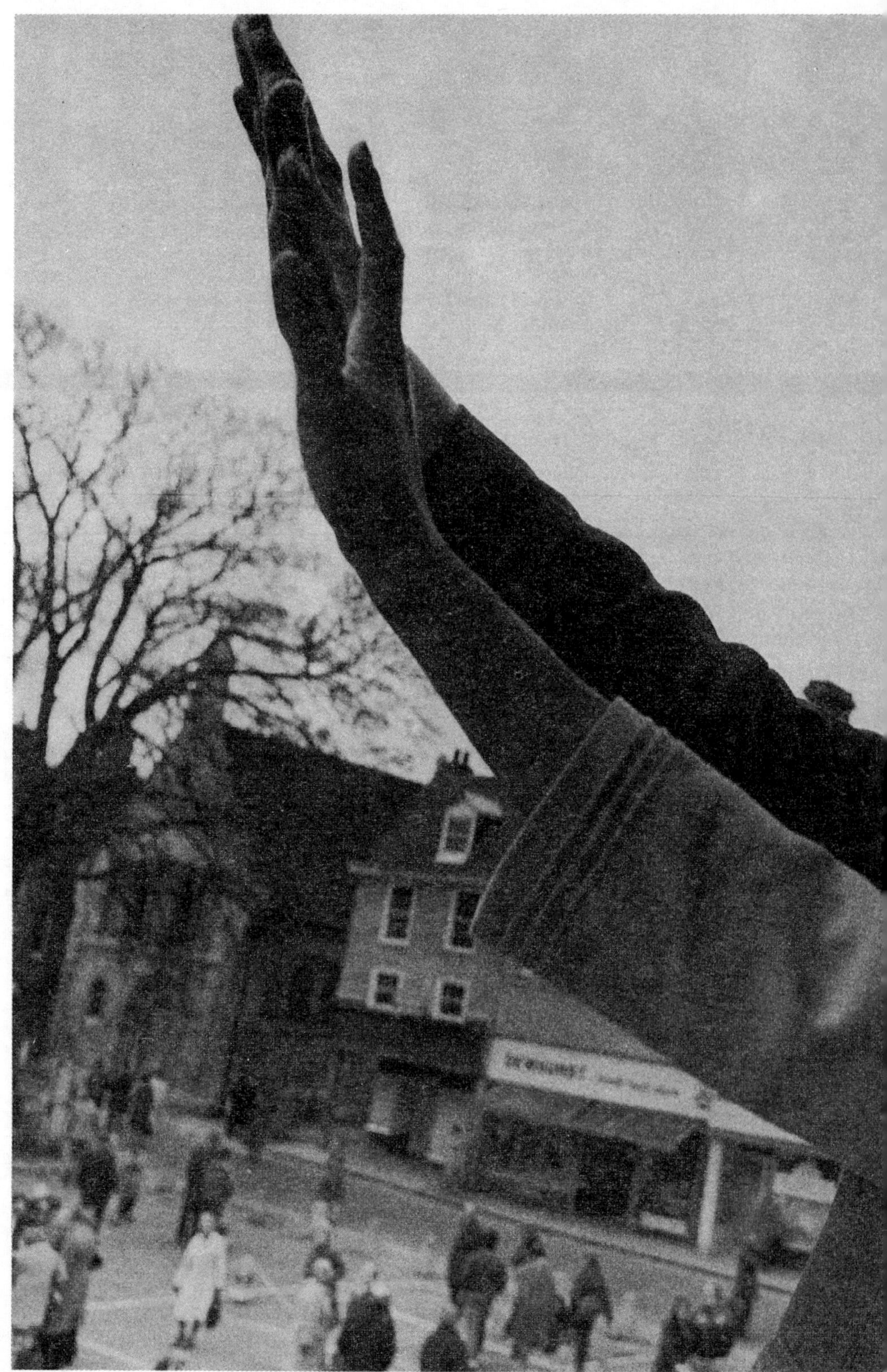

Major in with massive majority

Huntingdonshire voters turned out en masse to put the Conservative candidate, Mr John Major, in Parliament with a 21,563 majority.

On a 76.8 percentage poll – described as enormous – Mr Major, aged 36, a married man with two children, captured more than half the total votes cast.

The three main candidates said they were "shocked" at the size of the vote cast for the National Front candidate, Mr Kenneth Robinson, who polled 983.

The Labour vote for Mr Julian Fulbrook was up by just under 1,000 on the1974 election while the Liberal candidate, Mr Dennis Rowe, had to be content with third place and a drop of just under 3,000.

Mr Major received a massive 40,193 votes – more than doubling the 9,244 majority of Sir David Renton, who retired before the election after representing the constituency for 24 years.

Mr Major said: "I am very proud indeed about being elected. I did not expect a majority of this size. I was surprised and shocked at the National Front vote but it is heartening to see that nationally the National Front vote is derisory."

CAMBRIDGE EVENING NEWS

It was third time lucky when John Major stood for election to the Huntingdonshire constituency in 1979. Two fruitless battles in the safe Labour seat of Camden, St Pancras North in 1974 brought the expected heavy defeats, but it would have been a disaster of cataclysmic proportions if he had not held the Huntingdonshire seat for the Tories. In the event, he doubled his predecessor's majority.

A wave to the crowds in the 1979 General Election.

HUNTINGDONSHIRE

Electorate 93,862 1974: 79,724

Major, J. (C)	40,193
Fulbrook, J. (Lab)	18,630
Rowe, D.G. (L)	12,812
Robinson, K. (Nat Front)	983
C majority	21,563

Mr John Major contested Camden, St. Pancras North in February and October, 1974. Senior business development executive of British overseas merchant bank, and Associate of the Institute of Bankers. B March 1943; ed Rutlish Grammar School. Member London Borough of Lambeth Council, 1968-71. Founded Lambeth Borough Young Conservatives in 1965. Chairman, Brixton Conservative Association, member management board of Warden Housing Association, National Union of Bank Employees.

THE TIMES

It was just a month after the election, at 7.06 pm on June 13, 1979, during a debate on the previous day's Budget resolutions, that John Major was called by the Speaker for his maiden speech to the Commons, a milestone for all new MPs.

Maiden speech

economy

John Major's maiden speech followed the traditional pattern with references to his constituency, but during his 16-minute Commons debut he also dwelt at length on financial matters.

According to the official report, Mr Major declared: "I believe that public opinion requires four things of the Government in terms of economic management. It requires them to cut taxes, to curb inflation, to create new jobs and, as far as possible, to maintain satisfactory public services."

He accepted that not all these things could be achieved at the same time.

"In order to create jobs and to maintain public services, it is necessary first to cut taxes and to curb inflation," he said.

He had his eye on the long term and looked forward to "the success of this Budget over a period".

Mr Major allied himself firmly with the Chancellor, Sir Geoffrey Howe, and with the new Prime Minister, Margaret Thatcher, in sticking rigidly to the economic priorities set out.

"If we back away from the cash limits and the economic management that we have set ourselves, we shall face a distinct change in economic policy," he declared.

Mr Major found that MPs listened to his maiden speech quietly and politely, but envisaged that in the future the going would get tougher.

"I am grateful to the House ... for its traditional indulgence to a newcomer," he said. "I appreciate it, but I shall not expect it – and I imagine I shall not receive it – on future occasions."

PRESS ASSOCIATION

"I find him a really unknown candidate on face value but when you know his background you can see why they picked him. Let's hope he turns out to be a Clark Kent figure."

Businessman at American Chamber of Commerce

HUNTS MP IN WEST BANK SHOOTING

Huntingdonshire MP Mr John Major escaped unhurt when he was caught up in a shooting incident between Palestinians and Israelis on the West Bank.

Mr Major was one of 11 MPs on a fact-finding mission to the Middle East who had to dive for cover when bullets started flying.

He telephoned his wife, Norma, at the weekend to break the news.

Mrs Major said today: "It was the first I'd heard about it. The line was bad and he didn't have very much time.

"It came as a shock but when I spoke to John he was obviously alright. There was no point in panicking in retrospect."

Mr Major and the other MPs have now moved on from the West Bank trouble spot to Beirut. "I am hopeful that now everything is alright," said Mrs Major.

The 1983 election campaign focused attention sharply on every move by the candidates. This brief story was just one of the results.

ON THE MOVE

His opponents need derive no comforting conclusions from the fact that the Conservative's Huntingdon candidate, John Major, is trying to sell his house in Hemingford Grey for £69,950. There is no intention of moving outside the district, says his agent, Sheila Murphy.

CAMBRIDGE EVENING NEWS

John Major was one of many MPs concerned about young people's involvement with cults, and anxious to see them outlawed.

Major campaign to kill off cults

"DANGEROUS" religious cults are trying to lure Cambridgeshire youngsters into their clutches, an MP has warned.

Huntingdon MP Mr John Major has launched a campaign to kill off "weird" pseudo-religious cults operating in Cambridgeshire.

Mr Major said he had been contacted by several worried parents in the Huntingdon area whose teenage children had been induced into cults.

He would not name the cults involved, but said two or three were now or had been operating recently in the county.

Mr Major was explaining why he had launched a bitter attack on such cults in a speech to St Ives Young Conservatives.

Mr Major told the "News" that a Cambridgeshire university student was lured into a cult in Australia and asked his parents to pay for a self-improvement course designed to equip him for life.

He was rescued from the cult by relatives in Australia and is now back in the county, said Mr Major, who declined to identify the family.

"He was not a lame duck, a chap with a wing down. These cults are dangerous and should not be trifled with. Often intelligent and able people are induced into membership of cults." Mr Major cited the case of a 19-year-old A-level student from West Cambridgeshire who handed over cash and had to be "snatched back" from a cult operating in Birmingham.

Mr Major, as a government whip, does not speak in the Commons but is fighting behind the scenes to help outlaw cults.

He has a file of about 12 separate cults and is urging fellow MPs to use Commons privilege and expose their activities.

Mr Major has also had talks with Home Office ministers to urge investigation of cults masquerading as registered charities to gain tax benefits.

CAMBRIDGE EVENING NEWS

Victory for John Major in the 1983 General Election.

At the time of the 1983 general election, John Major was ensconced as a junior member of the Government and voters in his re-named and redrawn constituency returned him to his post with an increased share of the vote.

HUNTINGDON
Electorate 76 668

*Major, J. (C)	34 254	62.4%
Gatiss, Mrs S. (L/All)	13 906	25.3%
Slater, M. (Lab)	6317	11.5%
Eiloart (Eco)	444	0.8%
C majority	20,348	37.1%
Total vote 54 921		
Turnout 71.6%		

Mr John Major, who was appointed a Government whip in 1983, was elected for Huntingdonshire in 1979; contested Camden, St Pancras North in Feb and Oct 74. Senior Executive of British Overseas Bank and associate of the Institute of Bankers. Born March 29 1943; educ. Rutlish Grammar School. Member, London Borough of Lambeth Council, 1968-71. Founded Lambeth Borough Young Conservatives in 1965. Chairman, Brixton Conservative Association, 1970-71. Chairman, Beckenham Conservative Association. Member, Board of Warden Housing Association, 1975-83. Former secretary, Conservative parliamentary party environment committee, PPS to Ministers of State, Home Office 1981-83.

THE TIMES

The Government Whips' office is widely seen as a fast track route to the higher echelons at Westminster. John Major's promotion came in the aftermath of the Brighton IRA attack on the Tory conference and while Major was helping out in the constituency of the Chief Whip, John Wakeham, who was seriously injured in the bombing.

New whip's post for Major

Promoted Huntingdon MP John Major will have twin responsibilities in his new post as a senior Government whip – for the Treasury and Northern Ireland.

Mr Major, 41, is one of five senior whips who each have special duties in different Government departments.

Prime jobs for Mr Major, who was elevated in the wake of the recent Government reshuffle, will be to see financial legislation and the Budget through the Commons.

Mr Major has a grounding in financial affairs – when he became a junior whip last year, he resigned as a senior executive with the Standard Chartered Bank.

His Northern Ireland duties, which are secondary to his Treasury job, will involve getting laws relating to the province through the Commons.

Mr Major was allocated the two responsibilities last week soon after his promotion was announced.

Earlier this week he travelled to Brighton to visit IRA bomb victims and the chief whip, John Wakeham, who is recovering from injuries in hospital.

Before his Treasury and Northern Ireland appointments, Mr Major's responsibilities as a whip related to the Department of the Environment.

Mr Major was elected in 1979 and during his five years in the Commons has had three promotions.

CAMBRIDGE EVENING NEWS

"The inexperienced Major is the young knight to whom the Iron Lady has entrusted the Holy Grail."

Dagens Nyheter, Swedish daily newspaper

Cruise village 'will not be another Greenham'

By JOHN SHAW

The Government had plans to prevent "another Greenham" at RAF Molesworth, the Cambridgeshire site of the second cruise missile base in Britain, Mr John Major, Conservative MP for Hunt- ingdon, told worried villagers at the weekend.

It had "learned a lot" from the protest at Greenham Common, Berkshire. "We didn't like what we saw there and after the fence is put up at Molesworth, arrangements will be made to prevent another Greenham in this area."

He declined to reveal details of the plans or when the eviction of 100 peace protesters already camped on the site would take place. Molesworth is to be the main target of CND activity.

"At a proper time, they will be removed, lock, stock and barrel – and chapel," he said in a reference to the stone peace chapel built by demonstrators at the airfield entrance.

"It isn't in the far distance and when we remove them we will do so in such a way that we'll prevent the return of others."

At present the former wartime American bomber base lacks even a perimeter fence. But construction work is due to start next year with the aim of making the airfield operational with 64 cruise missiles by 1988.

The site is in a very rural area and villagers fear that their way of life will be changed utterly by "peace protesters" and American servicemen.

Mr Major faced angry questions from residents who claimed the police were doing nothing to prevent alleged instances of drug possession, abusive language and indecent exposure by protesters at Rainbow Camp, one of two peace sites at Molesworth.

Mr Major, who also lives locally, said: "I don't like what the demonstrators are doing any more than you do. I will take any action I can within the law to see that they are removed decisively."

The meeting was attended by people from six villages plus a handful of protesters who included Mrs Jean Hutchinson, a veteran peace campaigner from St Ives, Cambridgeshire. She was escorted away by police after being refused the chance to speak.

DAILY TELEGRAPH

Bishop in Peace Protest

By JOHN SHAW

A BISHOP was at the centre of a row over cruise missiles after he said prayers at the opening of a new permanent peace camp outside the American base at Alconbury, near Huntingdon, yesterday.

The Rt. Rev. William Gordon Roe, Suffragan Bishop of Huntingdon since 1980, was invited to take part by camp organisers.

But his action was criticised by Mr John Major, Conservative MP for Huntingdon, and the residents of villages surrounding the airfield, a support centre for the proposed cruise missile base at RAF Molesworth.

Mr Major described the protesters' actions as "silly and futile gestures and very hostile towards the community. I regret that the bishop decided to attend because his presence will be misused by people in a fashion of which he will not approve."

The bishop faced further criticism from Mr Terry Pinner, chairman of the Stukeleys Parish Council, which covers the villages of Great and Little Stukeley whose residents have decorated the village signposts to read: "Little Stukeley does not welcome the peace campers."

Mr Pinner said: "The bishop would do better to spend his time finding a new parson for our parishes – something we have been without for some time. We live in a small community and we don't want these people interfering with it."

But the bishop, 62, said the protesters "needed all the support they can get".

Among the spectators was Mrs Emily Blatch, leader of the Conservative controlled Cambridgeshire County Council whose ward includes Alconbury. She said she would be taking legal advice to see what action could be taken against the group, with the possibility of obtaining a repossession order for the road verge occupied by the campers.

DAILY TELEGRAPH

'New Greenham' fear at second cruise base

By JOHN SHAW

"PEACE campaigners have disrupted the lives of villagers living around RAF Molesworth, the Cambridgeshire site of the second cruise missile base in Britain," said Mr John Major, Conservative MP for Huntingdon, yesterday.

They have been squatting in and around the 700-acre former wartime airfield for three years, but their numbers have increased in recent weeks to between 150 and 200, far more than at Greenham Common, Berks, the first cruise site.

A peace chapel has been partly built from oddments of bricks and timber and the protesters have now launched a roof appeal. The sudden establishment of a squatters' enclave is regarded with apprehension by the villagers who fear the area will become "another Greenham". Mr Major, whose constituency includes Molesworth and its villages, said: "I have a file of letters six inches thick from local people and there is overwhelming public opposition to the two peace camps."

The campers live in two muddy settlements on the fringes of the airfield, occupying tents and an assortment of old vehicles, usually single or double decker buses, whose windows are either painted or blocked off with cardboard.

A few have lived on the derelict, grass covered site since 1981, but the latest arrivals are from the Peace Convoy, a group which trails around pop festivals in the summer.

Mr Richard Beeby who farms 1,000 acres adjoining the airfield, said: "We are sick of them, absolutely sick of them. They have stolen my property consistently over the past three years and nothing seems to be done about it.

"I had £350-worth of wood taken last week. They are camping illegally and more are coming all the time. This used to be a lovely little place, with its own shop, pub and village hall. But now the shop is closing because of these people and the nearest is six miles away.

"The very presence of these campers frightens people. It is visual intimidation and I think a lot of the older folk find it menacing." Mr Melvyn Latchford and his wife, Jean, who have run the village shop and post office for two years, confirmed they had decided to close both businesses at the end of the month.

Asked if the peace camp presence was the reason, Mr Latchford said: "I would say it has got us both down. Trade started to decline because the locals would not come in since the peace people were coming to use the post office." A Cambridgeshire police spokesman said police were aware of complaints from the villagers and extra patrols had been mounted. There had been a number of prosecutions arising from incidents at the peace camp, he added.

A long-running controversy in John Major's constituency centred on the cruise missile base at Molesworth, the second British airfield to be designated as a home for the missiles after Greenham Common, Berkshire. At Greenham, women demonstrators maintained a permanent presence and had been supported by huge weekend demonstrations opposed to the siting of the missiles. The Molesworth protest ended in a mass eviction by police and troops on February 6, 1985.

Protest 'wired for sound'

AN MP yesterday demanded an inquiry into methods used by a TV crew to film a break-in at a Cruise missile base.

Sixteen anti-nuclear campaigners have been charged with trespass after using ladders to scale the 12ft. inner security fence at RAF Molesworth, Cambridgeshire.

Some were wearing concealed body microphones as they were filmed by Diverse Productions for the Channel Four programme Diverse Reports due to be screened next month.

John Major, Tory MP for Huntingdon which includes the base, wants the Independent Broadcasting Authority to investigate who provided the microphones and take disciplinary action if the crew did.

He said he would expect charges to be brought if the crew connived in illegal activities.

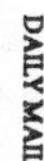

A heavily policed anti-Cruise missile demonstration at RAF Molesworth

2

Junior Minister

John Major was quick to make his mark in Parliament and reach the first rung of the ladder to higher things when he became a parliamentary private secretary to two junior Home Office ministers.

It wasn't long before promotion arrived, and he was appointed to the Department of Health, and then to a key role dealing with Social Security.

The complex and sensitive field was an ideal proving ground for John Major, with his eye for detail, his ability to absorb information, and his keen awareness of the political aspects of the job.

Big reshuffle in Thatcher's middle ranks

The Prime Minister dismissed seven ministers in a reshuffle in which 33 changes were announced.
A central theme was the strengthening of the Department of Health and Social Security.
One surprise was the appointment of Mr Peter Morrison as another deputy chairman of the Conservative Party.
Two women were promoted — Mrs Angela Rumbold to education and Mrs Edwina Currie to the DHSS

By Robin Oakley and Philip Webster

It was taken as a compliment to John Major from the Prime Minister that in order to strengthen the Social Security Department, she appointed him minister under the Secretary of State for Health and Social Security, in one of a series of changes designed to move the direction of her Government sharply to the right.

In the most extensive reshuffle of her two governments, the Prime Minister last night refashioned the middle ranks of her ministerial team for the run up to the general election.

The Cabinet was left untouched, but she dismissed seven ministers in 33 changes. There are further changes to come.

Only on the formation of her second government in June, 1983, has Mrs Thatcher pruned her ministerial team so comprehensively. Yesterday's reshuffle will please the Tory radical right but disappoint the "wets".

Mrs Margaret Thatcher considered changes at Cabinet level but quickly discarded the idea, believing that after the changes forced on her this year, a period of stability was needed.

But a central theme of the reorganisations was the strengthening of Mr Norman Fowler's Department of Health and Social Security.

Conservative Party chiefs had been alarmed at the success of the Labour Party's propaganda battle on health and Mr Fowler was reported to be delighted with the changes which move Mr Tony Newton, seen in Downing Street as a high-flyer, to the key post of Minister for Health. He replaces Mr Barney Hayhoe.

Mr John Major is promoted to Mr Newton's old job as Minister of State for Social Security. There are two well-regarded newcomers to the same department, the outspoken Midlands MP Edwina Currie and the Leading QC, Mr Nicholas Lyell.

As Tory backbenchers last night digested the changes, it was noted that the large majority of ministers dropped were of a leftish tinge while the lion's share of promotions went to the right.

Mrs Thatcher has been urged by her most faithful followers to

THE TIMES

John Major visiting a Community Health Council office in his Cambridgeshire constituency.

counteract the advance secured by the "wets" in last Autumn's Cabinet reshuffle and the smaller revisions that have taken place since. These included the elevation to the Cabinet of Mr Kenneth Baker, Mr Kenneth Clarke and Mr Malcolm Rifkind, and the promotion to the key post of Minister of State at the Foreign Office of Mrs Lynda Chalker.

John Major

Mr John Major's ministerial elevation will please MPs of all parties because he is widely regarded as one of the most likable Conservative politicians.

Aged 43, he is a middle of the road Conservative who over the past year was parliamentary under secretary at the Department of Health and Social Security.

Elected in 1979 at Huntingdon, the former banker was appointed a parliamentary private secretary to two Home Office ministers. In 1983, he moved to the Whips' office.

Opposite, *The Minister of State for Social Security.*

First day for promoted Major

There was already talk of higher things for the newly-promoted John Major when local MPs were consulted for their views of his promotion. But there was modesty in his response to the speculation.

HUNTINGDON'S MP Mr John Major – just promoted to social security minister – spent his first day in the job tackling next year's spending plans.

And today, Sir Anthony Grant, MP for South West Cambs, tipped Mr Major for a Cabinet post.

"I am absolutely delighted with John Major's promotion. He is not only a good friend and an excellent MP but he is undoubtedly one of the rising stars of this Government.

"I am sure he will go to the Cabinet in the future and I would welcome it," he said.

Competent

Sir Anthony was backed by former Foreign Secretary and defence minister Mr Francis Pym, MP for South East Cambridgeshire.

"I feel pleased for him because he is an extremely competent minister and he has a great future in politics," he said. "I hope he will make it to the Cabinet."

Mr Major, 43, of Great Stukeley, near Huntingdon, was told of his new post by the Prime Minister personally after yesterday's reshuffle. Today he told the "News" he was absolutely delighted: "It is an interesting job and one which I want to do.

"It is very generous of Mr Pym to say that but I think I had better do the social security job adequately first," he said.

Salary

In the coming year his task will be to implement the new Social Security Act and draw up new regulations which, he says, will affect 90 per cent of the population.

He was junior social security minister and a Government whip. Now, as social security minister, his salary rises to around £35,000 a year.

Mid-Bedfordshire MP Nick Lyell was also promoted in the reshuffle, to the social services team.

CAMBRIDGE EVENING NEWS

The annual Conservative conference provides more opportunities for young ministers to shine, and John Major's 1986 speeches were exactly what his audience wanted to hear.

Social Services

Fraud and abuse will be cut out

Social security cheats were given a warning by Mr John Major, Minister of Social Security and the Disabled. The Government was determined to cut out fraud and abuse. The money to help the needy came from the tax-payer, and it must be spent fairly, he said.

In the past year the Government had dealt with 100,000 cases and saved £120 million.

"That is good but not good enough so we are stepping up our actions," Mr Major told the conference. Another 500 staff had been appointed.

"Let me give this warning to the cheats. When we detect serious fraud we will not hesitate to prosecute." Money for the social security system was willingly given, mostly by those on modest incomes. The rich could not finance the programme if every penny they had was taken in tax. It was dishonest of Mr Roy Hattersley, the shadow Chancellor, to pretend otherwise.

Mr Major, speaking during a social services debate, bitterly resented the Labour slander that Conservatives did not care. They had a record of care and of cash, not of crocodile tears.

He said that Mr Michael Meacher, Labour's shadow health minister, travelled the country like a peripatetic Santa Claus littering uncosted promises with every speech. A Meacher speech was an expensive speech for he was a master of the blank cheque.

"He writes it, but the tax-payer pays it." He said that last week Mr Meacher promised to increase pensions effectively to one half or one third of average earnings for couples and single pensioners, respectively. That was desirable but the cost could be as much as £16 billion a year.

How would that be met? Borrowing would have ruinous inflationary consequences. And if the money came from the tax and national insurance payer it would increase national insurance, for example, by £14 a week for every person in work.

"It is, in short, an unachievable, cynical, bogus and dishonest promise."

The Government's new social security system would be simpler. Rates had not been finalized, but most disabled under pension age would gain over £200 a year. The conference carried, by an overwhelming majority, a motion commending the Government's reform programme for social security and calling on the Secretary of State for Social Services, Mr Norman Fowler, to ensure that benefits continued to be targeted towards those most in need.

THE TIMES

The second 1986 Tory conference speech.

Labour benefits pledge 'dishonest'

LABOUR'S promises to increase social security benefits were dishonest, and their costing of their proposed pension and child benefit changes was a £2 billion underestimate, Mr John Major, Social Security Minister, told the conference.

The promise by Mr Michael Meacher, Labour's social security spokesman, to increase pensions to one half and one third average earnings for couples and single pensioners respectively could cost as much as £16 billion a year, he said.

If that was paid for by extra borrowing it would have ruinous inflationary consequences. If it came from increased National Insurance contributions it would mean everyone in work would pay an extra £14 a week.

"The Labour Chancellor would have his hands in your pocket more frequently than you would," Mr Major said.

It is an unachievable, cynical, bogus and dishonest promise.

Conservative costings of the promise by Mr Roy Hattersley, the Shadow Chancellor, for pension and child benefit increases had shown that it was not £3.5 billion, as Labour said, but £5.5 billion.

Mr Major put forward his explanation of why the only costing in the whole programme was two thirds wrong as: "Roy Hattersley did the costing and he did it after lunch." Explaining his costing, Mr Major said that if Labour's estimate of £3.5 billion was right, it would mean the very poorest pensioner would get nothing at all.

How dare they

To prevent that would cost an extra £1 billion. If Labour followed their long-standing practice of increasing linked rates to the sick and others, the true cost became £5.5 billion.

Replying to a motion commending the Government for targeting benefits to those most in need, Mr Major said that in contrast the Government would not promise what it could not achieve.

As a result of the reform of social security most disabled people under pension age would gain over £200 a year, with many gaining much more.

Under the Conservatives, the tax on disabled people for the mobility allowance had been removed, as had the invalidity trap which had caught tens of thousands of sick and disabled.

Mr Major demanded, amid applause: "How dare they say we don't care for these people?" On retirement pensions he said: "Our commitment to the pensioner is absolute and it stands."

From next April pensions would be raised at the same time as the tax, rent and rate changes took place. That was why the interim up-rating has been 65p and 40p.

Chances reduced

There had been three benefit increases in 17 months and Mr Norman Fowler, Social Services Secretary, would soon be announcing another.

Although the motion was passed easily, some objection was taken in the debate to a reference to concentrating care on groups such as the heads of one-parent families.

Mr Anthony Breen (Norwood), a Lambeth councillor, said that in such boroughs, single women were advised that if they had a baby they would be rehoused automatically.

The chances for families on the waiting list for years were reduced accordingly.

Mr Brian Oxley (Sheffield Central) said, amid cheers: "What we must not do is encourage silly young girls to become one-parent families so they can go to the top of the waiting list and get their supplementary benefits."

DAILY TELEGRAPH

"Major would get up and say that we had to help people. Many of us on the left were acutely embarrassed about the previous record of Labour."

Ken Livingstone, commenting on their time as Lambeth Councillors

The long-running dispute at artificial limb makers J. A. Hanger was the target of several Opposition attacks on the Government, but Major strongly defended his position of non-intervention in a dispute between the management and its employees.

Legal challenge on Hanger dispute

The Government's position on the dispute at J.A. Hanger & Co., the Roehampton company that supplies artificial limbs, was legally unsound, Mr Frank Dobson, an opposition spokesman on health, said in moving an opposition motion regretting the interruption of service to severely disabled people.

He said that the contract for the supply and fitting of limbs was not between company and the people. It was between the company and the Government. Failure to provide a proper service was in breach of that contract. Yet still the Government refused to take resolute action to end the dispute which had been going on for 10 weeks and a day.

Three hundred skilled and hardworking staff who had followed agreed procedures and who were provoked beyond endurance were dismissed and the people they wished to serve put into difficulty.

The company was run by odious toads. DHSS ministers were craven and complacent and they would rather patients suffered and workers and their families went without offending the sort of company on which the Prime Minister doted. Mr John Major, Minister for Social Security, moved a government amendment urging the management and workforce to resolve the dispute without delay and noting with approval the Government's initiatives to minimise inconvenience to patients.

He said Mr Dobson had made a partisan, contemptuous, ill informed and mischievous picket line speech, which would do nothing to resolve the dispute.

This was an industrial dispute between the management and

THE TIMES

one part of its workforce and it could be resolved only by them.

The Government was not a direct party to the dispute but it was interested in patient care during and beyond the dispute.

He did not propose to intervene directly because such action might be counter productive and Acas existed for that purpose.

He had met the managing director of the company this morning to confirm that the company was doing everything possible to maintain the service to patients. He had been given an assurance that priority action was being taken and would continue to be taken in urgent cases.

Mr Jack Ashley (Stoke on Trent South, Lab) said this was one of the saddest disputes he had ever known because of its terrible impact on the disabled.

Dismissing workers for going on strike was outrageous. Dismissing the workforce and then agreeing to reinstate a proportion of it before negotiations was a certain recipe for prolonged industrial misery and it simply would not work.

Mr Terry Fields (Liverpool Broad Green, Lab) said he had been on the picket line and the morale among the workers was extremely high. Since the dispute had started, 23 people had left the factory. Only six had found jobs.

The average age of the workforce was between 40 and 50.

BTR, the parent company, had made £151 million profit through its investment round the world.

Victory for disabled

One piece of good news that John Major could give the Commons concerned an amendment to new social security regulations on severely disabled people after the original proposals had been widely criticised.

More severely disabled people will qualify for extra allowances under new arrangements announced by the social security minister, Mr John Major, yesterday.

From April 1988, when the social security reforms come into effect, severely disabled people living independently in the community will qualify for an extra premium even if they are currently receiving the lower rate of attendance allowance.

The announcement comes after widespread criticism of the original proposal that only those receiving attendance allowance at the higher rate would be eligible. Mr Major said that 7,000 people would qualify at a cost of £8 million.

THE TIMES

Tory revolt on jobless mortgage cash cuts

John Major's ideas for amendments to social security benefits did not always go down well within his own party. But, as on other occasions, the revolt petered out and the Government comfortably got its way.

by David Hencke, Westminster Correspondent

THE GOVERNMENT is set to face a Conservative backbench revolt tonight over its plans to allow benefit payments to cover only half of a newly unemployed person's mortgage interest for the first four months, after that person loses a job.

Plans by Mr John Major, the Social Security minister, to introduce the curbs appear to have angered a sizeable number of backbenchers, who feel they can not support the Government on the issue.

Mr Robin Squire (C, Hornchurch), one of five Conservatives who spoke out against the proposal last week, said yesterday: "I cannot conceivably see how a social security minister could have put this forward to save £23 million out of a budget increase of some £4 billion. It seems without rhyme or political reason." Conservative MPs blame the Treasury for insisting that the Department of Health and Social Security come up with some savings.

MPs yesterday were given a briefing from the National Council for One-Parent Families claiming that deserted wives will be one of the main losers in any change. Miss Sue Slipman, the director of the organisation, says that many single parents could be driven into homelessness by the rules when they are already facing chronic financial insecurity.

The organisation quotes two cases – a Mrs Marberry in Surrey and Ms Jane Derrick in Norfolk – who would have suffered if the new regulations were in force.

Mrs Marberry was left with £800 mortgage arrears when her husband deserted her and did not contribute any maintenance for her and her three children.

The building society was threatening to foreclose because it could not see how she could pay off her arrears. Under the DHSS rules she was allowed to keep £12 a week from her wages in a part-time job and slowly pay off the debt. Under the new rules her arrears would have jumped to £1,200.

Ms Derrick gave up her job when she became pregnant and was worried she would have been evicted because of mortgage arrears.

Under the new rules when only half her interest would initially be met she would either have to consider an abortion or face eviction.

Miss Slipman says to MPs: "We cannot believe that the Government could have intended to jeopardise family stability and add more separated, deserted, divorced and widowed mothers and their children to the ever-lengthening list of those who are homeless and forced into insanitary, temporary accommodation for indefinite periods."

THE GUARDIAN

ATTACK ON "SCROOGE" MAJOR OVER MORTGAGE BENEFIT CUT

Locally two Cambridgeshire Labour candidates saw the chance to attack John Major over the mortgage benefit plan. But his mind was made up and he defended the plan briskly.

TWO Labour prospective parliamentary candidates have dubbed Huntingdon MP John Major the Scrooge of Christmas Present.

They blame the social security minister for the Government's plans to cut the mortgage interest relief of the unemployed.

Councillor Chris Howard, Labour leader of Cambridge City Council, and Cambridgeshire County Councillor Dave Brown, prospective candidates for Cambridge and Huntingdon, believe the £23 million saving is not justified and will not save money in the long run.

They say: "The £23 million saving is a miserly sum. The Tory decision to slash mortgage interest help for the newly unemployed is a classic case of kicking people when they are down.

"Only the most mean-minded of governments would add to the worries of those who have just lost their jobs by threatening them with the prospect of not being able to see a roof over their heads." They continue to say that 1987 is the Year of the Homeless yet the Government is welcoming it by cutting in half the mortgage interest relief for the first four months of unemployment.

They say that the measure could mean a sharp rise in repossessions and homelessness and this could actually cost the Government more than the £23 million it is saving.

Mr John Major does not accept the charges and believes the measures, while making the saving, should not cause any hardship. He said: "It sounds like Mr Howard and Mr Brown are up to their old tricks of creating stories to scare people which have no basis in fact."

Mr Major said the cut in relief would only apply for 16 weeks, during which time the Government would only pay half of the mortgage interest.

"Both the building societies and the social security advisory committee have said it will not cause any increase in repossessions." He said there are safeguards and that the building societies are unlikely to foreclose on what amounts to eight weeks' interest. He said they will regard it as an additional debt if the person is unable to pay their half of the interest.

He defended the £23 million saving: "It is justifiable and is not a miserly sum. It is a sum which can be well used in the social security budget."

CAMBRIDGE EVENING NEWS

The emotive issue of the disadvantaged, particularly the old and homeless, suffering the bitterly cold winter of 1987 brought a sustained attack from the Opposition and pressure groups. The trigger point for extra benefits was too low, they said, and the Government was not doing enough to help. A crisis meeting at Downing Street, chaired by the Prime Minister, decided that a Major plan to ease the situation should be adopted and he was able to announce the solution to the problem to the House of Commons.

Cash pledge to homeless after Commons row

By Richard Evans, Political Correspondent

As the death toll from the cold weather rose yesterday, the Government promised to pay for emergency shelter and food for the thousands of homeless people who have been sleeping rough and facing the worst of the freeze.

As politicians clashed in the Commons over ministers' handling of the crisis, the Government also undertook to study the possibility of opening up three Underground stations in Central London at night to give "dossers" a place to sleep.

Mr John Major, the Minister for Social Security, who is coordinating help for the old and cold, made an appeal to the fit and healthy to keep an unobtrusive eye on vulnerable neighbours and alert emergency services when necessary.

It is estimated that 25,000 to 40,000 people in London are homeless, and Mr Major told MPs that the Government would underwrite the additional expense incurred by voluntary organizations and charities who provide them with food and shelter.

By last night four government night shelters were due to have been opened up to provide extra room. Those who refuse to go into the emergency accommodation and insist on sleeping in the open will be provided with sleeping bags and food, with the Department of Health and Social Security paying the bill.

The action outlined by Mr Major came at the end of a stormy parliamentary debate in which Labour MPs repeatedly interrupted and clashed with the minister, who at one stage told a Labour back-bencher to stop "prattling like a constipated parrot".

Mr Neil Kinnock, the Labour leader, described by Mr Major as leader of the "yobbo tendency", jumped to his feet and angrily accused the minister of making inferior debating society points while cold and poor people outside were dying. "He plainly doesn't give a damn," Mr Kinnock said.

Mr Michael Meacher, the shadow social services secretary, who opened the debate, set the tone when he launched a bitter attack on the Government, particuarly criticising its exceptionally severe

THE TIMES

weather (ESV) payments scheme which only comes into operation when temperatures average below – 1.5C for a week.

Last week 14 weather stations registered average weekly temperatures below freezing and almost everywhere in the country was at freezing point, yet only a handful of payments were made. Mr Meacher said the scheme had been cynically devised to keep payments to minimum. "The scheme is virtually useless as it was intended to be." He said: "This scheme is hopelessly inadequate and has got to be replaced urgently."

Mr Meacher called on the Government to:

Scrap the ESV payment scheme and promise to pay £5 a week throughout the winter to 1.75 million pensioners on supplementary benefit and 1 million pensioners on the margins of poverty.

Open up Underground stations at Bank, Monument and Charing Cross to provide shelter for the homeless.

Provide an "adequate pension".

MPs rejected a Labour motion condemning the Government's handling of the cold weather payments policy by 335 votes to 190, a majority of 145. A Government amendment praising the level of provision for vulnerable groups was carried by 332 votes to 185.

Freeze not a crisis for the old, he says

By DAVID BRADSHAW and JOHN McSHANE

A TORY Minister was bitterly attacked yesterday after insisting that there is no crisis over old people dying from the cold.

Labour leaders and health care experts accuse him of "shameful and breathtaking complacency".

Social Security Minister John Major said at the weekend there were "only 643 deaths a year" involving hypothermia.

He said often hypothermia wasn't the main cause of death and the problem had been exaggerated in the past week.

The number of cases was dropping, he claimed.

But Shadow Health Secretary Michael Meacher said the Government was "writing off 643 people as though they were minor statistics".

He said: "It is an appalling indictment of their lack of concern and compassion."

Flooded

Malcolm Wicks, director of the Family Policy Studies Centre and author of Old And Cold, said the statistics included only cases where hypothermia was noted on the death certificate.

The number would run into thousands if heart, breathing and circulation – problems made worse by the cold – were counted.

Help the Aged said they had been flooded with calls from pensioners unable to cope.

Labour wants the £5-a-week "severe weather" allowance replaced with an automatic payment throughout the winter to those in need.

DAILY MIRROR

Minister denies cutting cold weather benefit

By Richard Evans, Political Correspondent

The Government last night denied cutting back on life-saving cold weather payments to the elderly as Britain became gripped by the worst weather this winter.

Age Concern and other pressure groups have bitterly criticized a new government scheme which provides that "exceptionally cold weather" payments of £5 a week are only paid when the average temperature throughout a week drops below minus 1.5C.

With biting cold winds and plummeting temperatures hitting Britain at the weekend, it was claimed that the new system would cut the amount of cash given to the elderly, and increase the risk of people dying from hypothermia.

But Mr John Major, Minister for Social Security, said: "The new scheme is not designed to produce a cut in public expenditure, nor will it." He said that more than £12 million was paid out in severe weather payments last year.

"We anticipate the new system will deliver the same level of help as in previous years, but it will be better targeted to the most vulnerable groups, such as those aged above 65, the chronically sick and disabled, and parents with young children under two.

"The scheme meets what we were asked to produce last year by pressure groups and others. It has clear criteria for payment, a known level of benefit to be delivered, and it is a better system for the claimant to understand." Under previous regulations, payments were triggered by weather that was exceptionally cold for a particular area. But that often meant payments were not made in Scotland and the north, in spite of having the coldest weather, while they were triggered in the south.

Mr Major said: "In the colder parts of the country the new scheme would have triggered payments in three of the last five years." Mr Major refuted claims that a single day of warm weather during a long bout of cold weather would cancel the right to payment. "You could have four cold and three relatively warm ones, but if the average temperature for the week was minus 1.5C then payments would be triggered." The exceptional cold weather cash is in addition to heating allowances totalling £400 million a year which are made to vulnerable groups.

Mr Robert McCrindle, Conservative MP for Brentwood and Ongar, and vicechairman of the party's health and social security committee, who urged the Government to reform the cold weather payments system, said last night he would be disappointed if the new system failed to give more money to more old people.

But if in practice many old people did not appear to be receiving the help they needed to heat their homes, he would press for a flat rate payment to all pensioners on supplementary benefit.

Cold cash level raised

By Richard Evans,
Political Correspondent

Severe weather payments to the "old and cold" will be made when the average temperature reaches freezing point – rather than minus 1.5C – Mr John Major, Minister for social security, told the Commons last night.

The change, which was immediately hailed as a Government climbdown by Labour MPs, came after a Downing Street meeting on Monday involving Mrs Margaret Thatcher, Mr Major and Mr John MacGregor, Chief Secretary to the Treasury.

The extra payments resulting from the raised temperature threshold are likely to cost up to £15 million.

Mr Major also told MPs that the exceptional cold weather payment of £5 will again be automatically made available this week to the 1.5 million people entitled to it before it is known if the temperature trigger point is reached.

Although Britain suffered the coldest temperatures for decades last week, returns from 64 weather stations round the country revealed that the average temperature for the seven days did not fall below minus 1.5C in 14 areas, most of them in Scotland, and so would have prevented many people from claiming the heating cash if the Government had not promised the automatic payment.

But in the Commons, Mr Major insisted the reason for changing the temperature trigger point was to give vulnerable groups the confidence to turn their heating up and keep warm. He was worried that many pensioners feared the minus 1.5C level would not be reached.

His announcement delighted Conservative back benchers who congratulated him for his sensitive, compassionate and flexible approach but Mr Michael Meacher, Labour's shadow social services secretary, said the climbdown was aimed at avoiding a weekly political dispute rather than guaranteeing warmth for the elderly.

In Wolverhampton, the Labour led council prepared to hand out £500,000 of rate-payers' money in one-off payments to 25,000 of the area's most needy pensioners to help with heating bills.

THE TIMES

Major answers cold weather cash critics

It was a rueful John Major who told the Cambridge Evening News *of "mischievous" reporting in the dispute over cold-weather payments, but he accepted the realities of his job, acknowledging that benefit cuts made good news stories for the media while improvements to benefit levels were unlikely to get the same publicity.*

When the temperatures plummeted and concern for the elderly grew, it was John Major who faced most of the criticism from the Opposition.

With announcements about the £5 cold-weather payment and the raising of the temperature at which the old and handicapped qualify for the money, rarely a day went by when he was not appearing on television or featured in the national newspapers.

Not all the publicity has been good – especially in the Sunday Times, which accused him of lacking sympathy.

Understandably, he is not pleased with the article in which that remark appeared.

He describes it as a "mischievous piece of reporting".

The MP angrily denies assertions that about 16,000 people a year are dying from hypothermia. He says the figure is actually 613 and that, among these, it was rarely the sole cause of death.

Mr Major describes as a "lurid concept" the idea of people freezing to death in their own homes unless they are seriously ill or perhaps have collapsed.

He does not accept that public opinion may regard him as hard-hearted. "I haven't had a single letter saying that I am unsympathetic," he said.

"The scheme was only in operation for four weeks and people were saying that –1.5 degrees was a bit low to trigger the payments. But it did trigger them twice: quite spectacularly across the whole country. So much for them saying we were trying to rig the system." He blames his opponents for scaring people into not turning their heating up and says that was one of the reasons for raising the qualifying temperature. "It was to make sure people had the confidence to turn up their heating." There are fundamental differences between his work as Government Whip and his new role, and he is very conscious of them.

"I can be absolutely certain if I announce a reduction in benefits there will be a lot of publicity, and I can be absolutely certain that if I announce an increase there will be very little publicity," he says.

Mr Major regards his current "visibility as just part of my job" but because of the heavy workload he has not even seen himself on television although he has done many interviews recently.

He sees himself staying at the DHSS for the time being but is tight-lipped about future portfolios.

"I just don't know. We will have to wait and see," he says.

If given the chance, 43-year-old Mr Major relaxes by reading, watching cricket or boating on the Ouse. He spent last weekend with his wife, Norma, and their two children at home in Great Stukeley before setting off for another week dividing his time between the DHSS and the House of Commons.

Mr Major is unlikely to be out of the news for long, even apart from his work at the DHSS; his constituency work involves him in the implications of the proposal to place Cruise missiles at RAF Molesworth.

CAMBRIDGE EVENING NEWS

John Major was forced to take responsibility for another disruption of the smooth running of the Government's legislative programme when he had to admit that there was a "technical error" in a new Act.

MINISTER ADMITS TO ERROR IN RULES FOR GRANT PAYMENTS

By Nicholas Wood, Political Reporter

Mr John Major, Minister for Social Security, who has been at the centre of the controversy over cold weather payments, admitted to the Commons yesterday that there is a mistake in the new Act changing the rules for payment of death and mater- nity grants.

Accepting responsibility for the "technical error", he told MPs that a short Bill putting matters right would he brought before the House today, and enabling the switch to the new system to go ahead from April 1.

The error, noticed by the Joint Committee of Statutory Instruments, arose because last year's Social Security Act did not give ministers the power to specify the size of the new payments.

MPs reacted with a mixture of derision, anger and outrage at the minister's statement, which came after last month's admission by Mr Nicholas Ridley, the Secretary of State for the Environment, that the £65 billion paid out in rate support grant over the past six years had been done so illegally, an oversight that led to the Local Government Finance Bill guillotined by the Government yesterday.

Mr Michael Latham, Conservative MP for Rutland and Melton and a member of the all-party Public Accounts Committee, drew support from all sides of the House when he told Mr Major that MPs were tiring of such confessions.

"Will my right honourable friend tell his draftsmen that the House of Commons is getting fed up with these errors and that if the draftsmen cannot get it right, they need not expect their CBs in the honours – rather we can put the work out to contract?" Mr Charles Kennedy, Alliance social security spokesman, sympathized with Mr Major, saying the he was "suffering from the onset of the political condition doctors now call Ridleyitis".

Mr Gordon Wilson, SNP MP for Dundee East, added: "While the minister very generously accepts responsibility for the follies and foolishness of his lawyers, does he not think it time that the DHSS sacked the lot of them and exposed them to the market economy in view of their failure to deal with the job given?" Mr Major said the original Bill had been substantial, technical and difficult and that he suspected similar errors had occurred in the past.

Mr Michael Meacher, the Opposition social security spokesman, claimed the "botch-up" had only happened because ministers were so anxious to overturn the Lords amendments and to rush it through Parliament before last summer's recess.

After the climbdown over cold weather payments and the "shambles of repeated court action over the illegal board and lodging regulations", the latest announcement only "enhanced the Government's growing reputation for bungling ineptitude", Mr Meacher added.

Mr Major retorted that the Labour MP should not be so critical of mistakes because he rarely got anything right himself. The last Labour Government had left the amounts of both grants unchanged.

Under the new system, the £25 maternity grant and the £30 death grant for help towards funeral expenses are abolished.

Instead, only low-income families claiming supplementary benefit, family income support or housing benefit will be entitled to assistance.

The maternity grant goes up to £80 and the "reasonable specified costs" of a funeral will be met from the new social fund.

Payouts running to several hundred pounds are anticipated.

In the case of a claim for funeral expenses, it is paid to a "designated person" subject to the proviso he or she is receiving benefit and does not have more than £500 in the bank.

Mr Major told MPs that under the new system payments would be targeted on those most in need rather than spread thinly across the whole population.

THE TIMES

Within days of a solution to the problem of cold-weather payments, widely seen at the time as the work of the Prime Minister, but achieved through an idea of John Major's, there was more trouble for the Social Security Minister over the delay in implementing a widely-approved act to help disabled people.

Major sits tight on aid to the disabled

By Brian Deer
Social Affairs Correspondent

JOHN MAJOR, the minister overruled by Mrs Thatcher in the "old and cold" £5 weather payments row, is facing a new challenge over his department's failure to implement an act of parliament that was meant to transform the lives of disabled people.

The Disabled Persons Act was approved by the Commons last April after winning all-party backing. Its aim was to create a national programme to assess the needs of disabled people, which would help them live in the community without recourse to institutions.

Under the act, which was proposed by Tom Clarke, Labour MP for Monklands West and the party's Scottish social services spokesman, some 5.5m people with physical or mental disabilities gained a right to have their needs assessed by their local council.

This could lead to:

Disabled children who leave special schools at the age of 16 to 19 being selected for day centre places or training.

Families caring for disabled relatives becoming entitled to home helps and other community services.

An end to the unplanned discharge of disabled people from hospitals into the community, which can lead to them living in substandard housing, sleeping rough or being readmitted to institutions.

"This was a very welcome act and it got support from all sides," said Peter Thurnham, Conservative MP for Bolton, this weekend.

But social services ministers have not produced the legal orders necessary for the act to take effect. According to Major, who is minister for the disabled as well as for social security, the Treasury will not provide the money and so the government will leave the core of the act dormant.

Full implementation of the act could eventually cost £150m a year, with £50m being spent on the post-education arrangements alone, but Major has indicated that he is willing to consider only about £5m worth of changes.

At the time of last year's Commons debate, ministers had planned to remove most of the act's crucial provisions.

But after considerable public support for the measures, key government amendments were withdrawn and a plan to "talk out" the act was abandoned by Conservative whips.

Now, organisations campaigning for disabled people believe that Major is masterminding a new means of killing the act without attracting criticism.

SUNDAY TIMES

The Hanger's dispute continued, but solutions to the problems of the affected patients had been found, and only the left wing still urged the Government to resolve the dispute.

MINISTER IGNORES HANGER'S WORKERS

By TONY CLARK

SOCIAL Security Minister John Major announced a shakeup to the artificial limb supply industry yesterday but failed to solve the long-running Hanger's dispute.

He told the Commons that the government is to act on a 13-month report into the service.

A special Health Authority is to be set up to oversee the industry, which is to be diversified, competition encouraged and a quicker and more flexible service provided than the existing near monopoly, he said.

But Labour MP Dennis Skinner pointed out that the 300 sacked Hanger workers at Roehampton also want an efficient service and their jobs back.

"Why does he (Mr. Major) not go down there and tell the management it wants the limbs produced more quickly and the way to do it is to get these men and women back at Hanger's?"

MORNING STAR

Finding out more about the problems facing old people.

John Major won the biggest Conservative majority in the country as part of Mrs Thatcher's 1987 landslide general election victory. And in the weeks before the election, Norma Major had cause for celebration too when her biography of Joan Sutherland – 11 years in the writing – was finally published.

Chance chat leads to opera star biography by Norma Major

IT HAD never been one of Norma Major's ambitions to write a book.

In fact when she looks at the first copies of the biography she has written – published this month – she still does so with a feeling of disbelief.

An essentially shy, unassuming woman, she has a busy life as an MP's wife – she is married to Huntingdon's MP, John Major – as well as looking after their family and home.

Her book, 11 years in the writing and the authorised biography of opera star Joan Sutherland, happened as a result of a chance conversation.

It was soon after the death of Maria Callas that Mrs Major, an opera-lover, was talking to a friend about the number of her performances. They moved on in their conversation to the Australian star, Joan Sutherland, whose singing she has loved since hearing the first note.

Free time

And they realised as they chatted that there was no catalogue of her performances.

At the time Mrs Major was looking after her two small children – Elizabeth is now 15 and James, 12 – and had little

HUNTINGDON
Electorate 86,186 (76,668)

*Major, J. (C)	40,530	63.6%
Nicholson, A.J. (SDP/All)	13,486	21.1%
Brown, D.M. (Lab)	8,883	13.9%
Lavin, B. (Grn)	874	1.4%
C majority	27,044	42.4%

Total Vote 63,773
Turnout 74.0%

No Change
Swing SDP/All to C 2.7%

Mr John Major was appointed Minister for Social Security and the Disabled, with the rank of Minister of State at the DHSS, in 1986; Under Secretary of State for Social Security, 1985-86; a Lord Commissioner of the Treasury (Govt whip), 1984-5; asst Govt whip, 1983-84. Elected for this seat, 1983; MP for Huntingdonshire, 1979-83; contested Camden St. Pancras N, Feb and Oct 74. Executive Standard Chartered Bank, 1965-79; Associate of the Inst of Bankers. B Mar 29 1943; ed Rutlish GS. Member, Lambeth BC, 1968-71; board of Warden Housing Assocn, 1975-83. Jt. sec Cons back bench environment committee, 1979-81. PPS to Ministers of State, Home Office, 1981-83. Parly consultant, Guild of Glass Engravers, 1979-83. Pres, Eastern Area YCs, 1983-85.

THE TIMES

free time. But she did send out many letters asking for details of Sutherland performances.

In response she found herself inundated with far more information than she needed. Many of the writers commented that it was about time there was another book about Joan Sutherland.

"It grew from that," said Mrs Major. But her commitments as a mother and political wife meant that the book always went to the bottom of the priority pile.

In that time Mrs Major, who is 45, has moved house three times and decorated two homes as well as helping her husband fight two General Elections. And she has always assisted with his correspondence.

But she did spend hours researching her subject in libraries.

"I always enjoyed working on the book and I grabbed it whenever I could," said Mrs Major, whose home, Finings, is just outside the village of Great Stukeley and within her husband's constituency.

Political Life

A domestic science teacher before she married her then banker husband, she enjoys the homemaking skills. She completely redecorated the family's present home herself, she makes clothes and embroiders and would not want domestic help in the house.

Quietly charming, she is not a person who would ever court publicity for herself. As an MP's wife she never makes speeches. Her husband is now Under Secretary of State for Social Security and she supports him whenever she can.

Fascinated by political life – she and her husband collect political biographies, particularly of prime ministers – she admits to having been terrified in the early days at the prospect of some of the functions she was called upon to attend.

"I would think I'm not going to get through the evening – going into a room with hundreds of people and I can't remember their names," she said. But it was always easier than she had feared.

Demanding Years

Studying Joan Sutherland's life – the opera star has given more than 2000 performances, she found herself wondering just how the singer managed to cope during some of her most demanding years with all the travelling to many different performances and learning new roles.

Last year Mrs Major, well aware that a General Election was in the offing, decided that her book must first be finished.

And that is just what she has done. Her biography, called Joan Sutherland, is to be launched this month. It is published by Macdonald Queen Anne Press at £12.95.

It has been tough on the family, she said – her children are day pupils at Kimbolton School – but it hasn't hurt them.

In many ways the production of the book has been like the arrival of a new baby. "But it has been a long, painful labour." Nowadays the Majors don't have as much time as they would like to go to the opera – her husband, too, lists it as one of his hobbies.

And there are other more pressing concerns at the moment. The family freezer is packed full of home cooked food labelled General Election. Early in the year, Norma Major prepared enough meals to last two or three weeks. Book launched, meals prepared, now when the crucial day is announced she will be free to throw herself into the campaign.

CAMBRIDGE EVENING NEWS

3

Cabinet Minister

The 1987 general election saw Margaret Thatcher returned to power with a landslide majority and gave her the wherewithal for sweeping changes to her Cabinet.

One of the beneficiaries was John Major, who was given the task of policing Government spending in his role as Chief Secretary to the Treasury.

The official confirmation of John Major's achievement of Cabinet rank.

PRIME MINISTER'S OFFICE
10 Downing Street, London, S.W.1

MINISTERIAL AND OTHER SALARIES ACT

In accordance with the provisions of Part VI(2) of the above mentioned Act, it is hereby notified with effect from 13th June 1987:

(1) The Right Honourable Kenneth Harry Clarke, Q.C., M.P., ceased to be Paymaster General upon his appointment as Chancellor of the Duchy of Lancaster.

(2) The Right Honourable Norman Beresford Tebbit, M.P., ceased to be Chancellor of the Duchy of Lancaster and a member of the Cabinet.

(3) The Right Honourable William John Biffen, M.P., ceased to be Lord Privy Seal and a member of the Cabinet.

(4) The Right Honourable John Roddick Russell MacGregor, O.B.E., M.P., ceased be Chief Secretary to the Treasury upon his appointment as Minister of Agriculture, Fisheries and Food.

(5) The Right Honourable John Major, M.P., became a member of the Cabinet on his appointment as Chief Secretary to the Treasury.

LONDON GAZETTE

The seemingly effortless rise of John Major continued after the June '87 General Election when Mrs Thatcher was returned to power with a thumping majority of 144. Despite the unpopularity of the job of Chief Secretary, his appointment was widely welcomed in political circles.

Watchdog at the Treasury

By our Political Staff

JOHN MAJOR, MP for Huntingdon, completed a meteoric rise to the Cabinet at the weekend when Mrs Thatcher appointed him Chief Secretary to the Treasury.

As deputy to Mr Lawson, Chancellor of the Exchequer, his main responsibility will be public spending, the annual round of haggling over which begins shortly.

Tall, bespectacled and quiet-spoken, Mr Major, 44, was voted the "man most likely to" by his contemporaries in the 1979 intake of Conservative MPs and is the first of them to reach the Cabinet.

He owes his promotion after nine months as Minister of State for Social Security to firmly held Right of Centre views which his manner belies, and a trenchant debating style which surprised Labour MPs who first experienced it last winter during the storm over cold weather payments for pensioners.

Mr Major also possesses a quickness with figures which he brought from his previous career in banking, a "street wisdom" from his Brixton childhood which he used to good effect as a Government Whip, and an ability to cut through red tape which served him well at the Department of Health and Social Security.

Teaming up with Mr Lawson, who is reckoned by colleagues to have had a "very good election", Mr Major's first task will be to help to pilot the remainder of the Finance Bill through the Commons. Only the bare bones of the measure reached the Statute Book before the election.

He will also be involved in negotiations over next year's Rate Support Grant – a highly contentious issue in counties like his own – and will then embark on the opening stages of the public spending exercise.

Despite his experience in the DHSS and an interest in both sides of its work, he is not expected to be a "soft touch" for demands for extra funding for health and social services unless they have advance Cabinet approval.

His task is the harder because during last year's review, Mr Fowler, the Social Services Secretary, pushed through an increase in the National Health Service budget which the then Chief Secretary, Mr John MacGregor, was politically unable to resist.

DAILY TELEGRAPH

One of a series of brief profiles of the new members of the Cabinet, summarising Major's potential and the difficulties he faced.

John Major

One of the new arrivals in the Cabinet, John Major has, in effect, become Minister for Cuts. His job as Chief Secretary to the Treasury is regarded as the most unpopular in the Government. While his predecessor's passage was eased by a slackening of the economic reins over health and education spending, Mr Major faces some tough bargaining, particularly with the Ministry of Defence.

He is eminently suited to a job which requires a grasp of the financial nitty-gritty. As a Government Whip, he saw the complicated Finance bill through the Commons and as Minister for Social Services, he tackled the fine detail of social security spending. He is acknowledged as a very bright facts and figures man.

Politically, the MP for Huntingdon is in the mould of Kenneth Clarke, a mainstream Conservative grammar school boy. He faces the difficult task of remaining genial and well-liked, while keeping a tight hold on the government purse.

THE TIMES

Tousle-haired and not in uniform, the future Cabinet Minister with his Wolf Cub pack in the early fifties.

The Cabinet after the 1987 general election.

John Major

JOHN MAJOR'S elevation to Chief Secretary to the Treasury will have surprised no one, least of all fellow Tory MPs who have watched him steadily rise in the Prime Minister's esteem over the past few years.

The 44-year-old Huntingdon MP is a more moderate version of Norman Tebbit. He was raised in Brixton, left school at 16 and learned politics mainly on the hoof and as a matter of instinct.

He impressed Mrs Thatcher last winter when, as Social Security Minister, he cut through red tape to ensure that old people received extra heating benefits during the cold spell in January.

SUNDAY TELEGRAPH

JUNE 1987

John Major's reputation as a popular and likable MP meant that his promotion to the Cabinet was widely welcomed, particularly among MPs for neighbouring constituencies.

MPs' delight at Major Cabinet post

MESSAGES of congratulation have poured in from all corners of the region for new Cabinet member, Huntingdon MP, Mr John Major. Conservative colleagues say they are delighted with his promotion to Chief Secretary in the Treasury, just announced by Mrs Margaret Thatcher, and they predict that Mr Major, former Minister of State for social security and the disabled, could go on to greater things.

"I think the Cabinet will benefit so much from his ability, compassion and caring," said SouthWest Cambridgeshire MP, Sir Anthony Grant.

"It is a very important role and I think that there is a bright future ahead of him."

Cambridge MP, Mr Robert Rhodes James, added: "It is a reflection of all the exceptional work he has done in the offices he has held.

"It is a key post and will be quite a test, but I have every confidence in him."

Exceptional

Saffron Walden MP, Sir Alan Haselhurst, said: "He has handled a sensitive job well and has obviously impressed the Prime Minister especially with his ability to master the nitty gritty of financial detail. I think it is a very deserving promotion."

Newmarket's MP, Sir Eldon Griffiths, said Mr Major's success was a result of his diligence.

"His carefulness in dealing with social security matters has been most impressive. He is hardworking and effective," he said.

CAMBRIDGE EVENING NEWS

The victory speech in 1987.

Cabinet power boost for Thatcher trio: job share-out benefits Parkinson, Hurd and Major

By Robin Oakey and Philip Webster

"His fellow ministers are particularly intrigued by the new role accorded to Mr Major."

Mr Cecil Parkinson and Mr John Major have been given key new roles in the Cabinet machine in the aftermath of Lord Whitelaw's retirement. Mr Douglas Hurd, the Home Secretary, also gains an enhanced status.

In the redistribution of committee chairmanships previously held by Lord Whitelaw, Mrs Thatcher has underlined the workload he had assumed by spreading the roles widely. But in so doing she has given personal boosts to three possible contenders in a future leadership election.

Mr Parkinson, Secretary of State for Energy, has been appointed to chair the important subcommittee of the Cabinet's Economic Affairs Committee which deals with local government finance. Its lengthy deliberations each year culminate in the fixing of the Rate Support Grant settlement, which has extensive public expenditure ramifications.

It is regarded by ministers as one of Lord Whitelaw's most vital roles. The fact that Mrs Thatcher has passed the job to Mr Parkinson who is technically only 20th in the Cabinet pecking order, marks another important step on his way back up the ladder.

Mr Parkinson became a close confidant of the Prime Minister during his time as party chairman and remained in close touch with her throughout his period on the back benches. He returned in the reshuffle that followed the general election, after an absence of four years.

His fellow ministers are particularly intrigued by the new role accorded to Mr Major, who came into the Cabinet for the first time after the election as Chief Secretary to the Treasury.

Mr Major, who made a big impression conducting his first public expenditure round as Chief Secretary, is to have a new role involving the co-ordination of Government publicity. He will adjudicate between conflicting approaches from different Government departments and be responsible for overseeing Government publications and publicity efforts in specific areas. In particular, all proposals on pay will be publicised through him. It is a job which requires fine political antennae and the ability to spot potential banana skins a long way off. Whitehall sources were at pains last night to play down the scope of Mr Major's new role and said that his precise responsibilities were still unclear. But while he is clearly not taking on the role exactly as Lord Whitelaw left it, Mr Major is moving into a trouble-shooting role, a tribute to the speed of his advance as the most junior member of the Cabinet.

Mr Hurd has been given charge of a secret Cabinet committee which co-ordinates the Government's efforts to counter terrorism. One of the big issues the committee will face over the next months will be the implications for countering terrorism as European border controls are

THE TIMES

relaxed, as part of efforts to build a single European market with fewer impediments to cross-border trade. Mr Hurd has made plain his determination to resist any moves to scrap border checks.

Some ministers had expected Mr Hurd to be put in charge of the "H" committee on home and social affairs. That, as previously disclosed, has been given to Mr John Wakeham, Leader of the Commons and Lord President of the Council.

It is understood that Mr Hurd did not have ambitions to take over that committee, feeling that the weight of Home Office legislation coming before it would make it impossible for him to chair it.

Sir Geoffrey Howe, the Foreign Secretary, who became No 2 in the Cabinet pecking order when Lord Whitelaw departed, has not been given any big new Cabinet committees but he had not expected one. Since he is away so often as Foreign Secretary, and is so deeply involved in Europe, there would be no time for him to become more closely involved in domestic policy issues.

Mr Wakeham has also been given the chairmanship of the legislation committee, which draws up the Queen's Speech.

His star has undoubtedly risen since the election, when Mrs Thatcher lost some of her faith in him after a disastrous radio broadcast.

But the distribution of the prizes shows that Mr Wakeham is not to be accorded anything like the influence which Lord Whitelaw had.

One other Cabinet committee chairmanship which Lord Whitelaw held, that of the Aids committee, has already been passed to John Moore, the Secretary of State for Social Services.

There is no new Cabinet committee post for Lord Young, but this does not reflect any lessening of his links with the Prime Minister.

The departure of Lord Whitelaw is expected to give Lord Young a greater say in the economic committees of which he is already a member.

The period of coolness between him and the Prime Minister in November and December, which followed the controversy over the Tory party chairmanship, is now said to have ended.

Rt. Hon. John Major to keep close eye on Government spending

High-flying Huntingdon MP John Major will now be known as Right Honourable, after landing a job in the Cabinet.

Mr Major, just appointed Chief Secretary to the Treasury, has been made a Privy Counsellor.

The news came after he had been summoned to Buckingham Palace where he was told he would be given the status of Right Honourable.

Mr Major – who has clinched five other important promotions in the last eight years – was sworn in at a meeting with the Queen and council president, Lord Whitelaw.

"I am very pleased indeed. I am looking forward to the job enormously," said Mr Major, who romped home last Thursday with an election majority of more than 27,000. Mr Major, former Minister of State for Social

continued on page 68

Kenneth Baker

Nicholas Ridley

The sparring over the 1987 public spending round began in earnest as discreet briefings launched the propaganda war.

BAKER LINES UP WITH RIDLEY TO FIGHT TREASURY

By James Naughtie,
Chief Political Correspondent

The Government yesterday hinted at some flexibility in its spending target for next year, but not enough to avert a fierce battle between the Treasury and a number of powerful ministers.

The Cabinet reaffirmed the target for 1988-9 of £154.2 billion, and a statement was issued saying that the annual spending review would come as close as possible to that figure while continuing to reduce public expenditure as a proportion of national income.

It appears to be accepted that there will be some slippage, but the signs last night were that a bruising battle lies ahead, with Mr Kenneth Baker, the Education Secretary, and Mr Nicholas Ridley, the Environment Secretary, the main protagonists in the fight against the Treasury.

The Cabinet paper circulated by Mr John Major, Chief Secretary to the Treasury, told ministers that the preliminary bids received earlier this month were much too high and had to be scaled down considerably in the next few weeks.

The public spending white paper this year laid out plans for public spending to be 41.75% per cent of gross domestic product next year, a drop of 1 per cent on this year's projected outturn. It was clear when Mrs Thatcher answered a challenge in the Commons from Mr Hattersley, Labour's deputy leader, that the Government's determination to keep the percentage falling is to be the principal weapon in its armoury.

A number of ministers are arguing that election commitment means the figures must change. Mr Baker is asking for a significant increase in the planned education total of £15.7 billion which is only a cash increase of £100 million on this year's planned total.

As well as extra resources for the sweeping changes to be introduced in this parliamentary session he is arguing for more capital

GUARDIAN

---

continued from page 65

Security and the Disabled, was summoned to 10 Downing Street on Saturday afternoon following a call from Mrs Thatcher's Principal Private Secretary.

He takes over from John MacGregor – appointed with a salary of £45,000 – who moves on to become Minister for Agriculture.

Mr Major's old job has been taken over by another rising star, former Transport Secretary Mr John Moore.

Mr Major's new work will involve keeping an eye on ministers' spending. He said it was too early to say whether he would be making any changes.

But the 44-year-old, due to attend a briefing session yesterday afternoon, pledged that he would keep a "very close eye indeed" on tax payers' money.

"It is going to be a very busy job, but so was being Minister for Social Security," he said.

Mr Major, first elected Huntingdonshire MP in 1979, started his climb up the political ladder in 1981 when he became Parliamentary Private Secretary to ministers of state at the Home Office.

In 1985 he rose to junior minister as Under Secretary of State for Social Security and later became Minister of State for Social Security and the Disabled.

CAMBRIDGE EVENING NEWS

spending to deal with complaints about school buildings.

Mr Ridley wanted more, largely to extend the scope of urban development corporations.

When the star chamber of ministers is established in September, to adjudicate in outstanding disputes, it is likely to be Mr Baker and Mr Ridley who will be its most notable witnesses.

Labour's assault on the spending plans began within minutes of the Cabinet meeting closing when Mr Gordon Brown, the shadow chief secretary, said that the real spending total would be about £2 billion less than this year's because the inflation estimate would prove to be too low.

He said: "Once again we have prime ministerial commitment unsupported by cash and the rhetoric of inner city regeneration without the resources to make it possible."

In the Commons, Mrs Thatcher said that one casualty of the Government's continued tight rein on spending was to be the request for extra funds from Britain for the European Space Agency.

One view, right, *of a speech on inner-cities policy.*

TORY 'GO IT ALONE' SNUB TO HARD-UP

By ANTON ANTONOWICZ

FAMILIES faced with the problems of living in Britain's rundown inner cities got this cold message from the Government yesterday: You're on your own.

Treasury Minister John Major said that Thatcherism had given many people the chance to solve their own problems through effort and self sacrifice. Now it was time to do the same in the inner cities, he told a Tory women's meeting in Chislehurst.

"We will not succeed by spending money," Mr Major said.

But he admitted that eight years of Tory government had done little for crumbling urban areas.

Mr Major's self help message was slammed last night by Labour's inner cities spokesman Roland Boyes. He said: "The suggestion that people loaded with massive problems can solve them without Government or Council help is absolute bunkum nonsense of the highest order."

DAILY MAIL

A less emotional report of the same speech on solving the problems of the inner cities.

Treasury warning of budget controls on inner city cash

By Philip Webster, Chief Political Correspondant

The problems of the inner cities cannot be solved by throwing money at them, Mr John Major, Chief Secretary to the Treasury, said last night.

Mr Major, who is in charge of efforts to keep public spending next year as near as possible to the Treasury target of £154 billion, said that inner city difficulties could be tackled only by direct action to encourage local initiative and by giving people the opportunity to be self-reliant. The challenge for the Conservatives' third term was to bring greater freedom and responsibility to the people of the inner cities, he said.

Mr Major's remarks were a clear warning to his Cabinet colleagues that there will he no blank cheque for spending on inner city projects, in spite of the high priority given to the subject by the Prime Minister.

The Treasury is faced with departmental spending of more than £6 billion above the target for next year, much of which is associated with action aimed specifically at the inner cities.

Mr Major said that prosperity had returned to Britain because the Government was curing the British disease.

But it had not used medicine. Instead it had relied on the self-healing properties of individual and business initiative, giving people the opportunity and responsibility to solve their own problems.

"By working with the grain of human nature and not against it we have tapped a willingness to accept greater responsibility. We have enabled the British to cure their own disease. Individual effort and self-reliance have replaced paternalism," he said.

Mr Major said that, as with the British disease, the Government alone could not solve the inner city problem.

"We will not succeed by spending money. That was not how the British economy was transformed. In every year since 1982-83 public expenditure has taken a progressively smaller share of the GDP; in the same period the economy has grown at almost 3 per cent a year."

THE TIMES

JOHN MAJOR TIPPED AS PARTY LEADER

By Our Political Correspondent

Mr Tebbit, the Tory party chairman, yesterday tipped Mr John Major, Treasury Chief Secretary, as a future Tory leader. He said that Mr Major, currently in charge of the Government's review of public spending, might succeed him as the 'ordinary bloke' at the helm of the party. Mr Major, MP for Huntingdon, emerged into the public eye when Mrs Thatcher promoted him to the Cabinet in the post election reshuffle.

DAILY TELEGRAPH

Norman Tebbit was a key figure in the Tory Party of the mid-1980s, but the tragic injuries to his wife, sustained in the Brighton bombing of the Tories' conference hotel in 1984, led to his gradual withdrawal from politics at the highest level. He remained, however, a hugely popular figure in the party, and his endorsement of John Major was the first from a Tory heavyweight.

Norman Tebbit's tip about John Major's future prospects prompted this profile.

Lawson's officer i/c public spending

By Lindsay Vincent

JOHN MAJOR looked not one inch out of place last Wednesday in the ornate surrounds and clubbish atmosphere of the annual Mansion House dinner, where Nigel Lawson berated the Americans for their inactivity in bringing in measures to halt the global financial panic.

Major, Chief Secretary to the Treasury and architect of the Chancellor's autumn statement, was making his Square Mile debut as the man holding the keys to the Whitehall tills. But he is no stranger to the parish, even if he was largely a stranger to City fathers during his tenure at Standard Chartered, where he was a senior banking executive before entering national politics in 1979.

Indeed, for much of his time in government, Major has similarly been under a cloak of anonymity, at least as far as the great British public is concerned. But matters changed last month when Norman Tebbit, out-going chairman of the Conservative Party, tipped Major as a future Tory leader.

Major, at a stroke, melted into the foreground. His new position at the Treasury will ensure he stays there.

Tebbit reckoned Major could also succeed him as the party's ordinary bloke. Major, understandably, will not be drawn to comment on this endorsement, which might one day prove to be a millstone.

Critics already reckon that Major's Mr Nice Guy image could rebound on him; they even go so far as to argue that he is not a polished performer on television, the politicians' two-edged sword.

"I do not like personality politics," says Major. "If Disraeli had been on television, I'm sure he would have come across as a very slippery person. Gladstone might not have been much better and what if Lord Palmerston took his teeth out? I prefer people to be judged on what they do."

Grooming

Major, 44, is the first of the 1979 Tory intake to reach the Cabinet, and is unquestionably as ambitious as others in the front line of the party's new boys. Colleagues consider him both able and amiable and he has so far justified the grooming laid out for him by the Conservative hierachy.

Whitehall watchers had Major well focused in their sights before the Tebbit remark, not only because his generation is reckoned to be the source of the next Tory leader.

Greying, softly-spoken and unfailingly courteous – outside Parliament – Major is not readily identifiable as someone who, as a 16 year old in the early Sixties, mounted a soap box to preach the Tory gospel in the tough inner London suburb of Brixton. Major's father, who was born in England – where is something of a family mystery – was 66 when, unexpectedly, he fathered his second son.

Major's mother was brought up in Mrs Thatcher's home town of Grantham.

A one-time trapeze artist with a travelling circus, proprietor of a Vaudeville show and professional baseball player in Philadelphia during a sojourn in the Americas around the turn of the century, Major Snr proved a failed capitalist in his declining years and the family's fortunes suffered.

The family was forced to leave Surrey and live in two rooms in Brixton.

Incongruous

Major decided at an early age that socialism was not working and vowed to become a politician the day he went to Westminster, aged 13, as a guest of the late Marcus Lipton, for years the Labour

OBSERVER

stalwart in Major's then constituency of Lambeth. As soon as he was eligible, at the age of 16, Major joined the Conservative Party.

A reluctant pupil at Rutlish Grammar School, he left school at the first opportunity and drifted into labouring. The family needed the money. But working on building sites and belonging to the Conservative Party was something of an incongruous mix, so Major turned his eyes toward the City and banking.

Gaining a degree in banking was not as daunting a prospect as entering some other professions at the age of 22. After thumbing through a list of British banks with overseas interests, Major wrote to Standard Chartered and was offered a job.

A year later he was sent to Nigeria at the height of the Biafran war. He returned a cripple, injured not in the hostilities but in an horrific motor accident. Major spent a year in a Croydon hospital, reading cricket books, Agatha Christie and Trollope. The bank held a position open and he returned to Standard after his convalescence.

Major combined local politics with banking and became close to Lord Barber, one-time Tory Chancellor under the Heath Government and later the chairman of Standard. His relationship with Barber was no hindrance to his political aspirations, and after fighting lost causes, he was finally offered the plum Tory seat of Huntingdon in 1979.

In 1983 he moved up a gear to the Whips' office, where he attracted attention for his handling of the Finance and rate-capping bills. He later became Minister for Social Security, one of the more arduous jobs in Whitehall, as Norman Fowler endeavoured to push through his welfare reform programme. Having made his mark wrestling with the complexities and intricacies of a near £50 billion budget, Major was offered the Treasury – and the Cabinet – where he monitors the spending of every Government department.

A tough negotiator, he did not endear himself to all Ministers in the recent negotiations over spending. But he achieved the task that the Party set out in its manifesto. The Government borrowing requirement is the lowest for 17 years, below the level forecast in the last Budget.

He is at the right place at the right time. Government revenues have afforded Major some scope to direct increasing resources to where he feels they are most needed – health, education and the police – and conduct the financial engineering which will open the way for next year's planned tax cuts.

Major will not comment on the current financial turmoil, on Government policy towards the nationalised industries nor on matters that are outside his immediate province at the Treasury. He may be on the left of the party, but he needs no lessons in diplomacy.

Egg, sausage, bacon and chips, please. Oh, yes, . . . and brown sauce too.

Man in the news: the rising star of the new British meritocracy – John Major

John Major's broad-based appeal to the Tory Party as a whole was highlighted in this profile as he prepared to embark on the 1988 public spending round.

By Peter Riddell

JOHN MAJOR, the Chief Secretary to the Treasury, could be forgiven for looking somewhat distracted on Tuesday when piloting the second reading of the finance bill through the Commons. After a character- istically combative speech, he only had time to listen to the front bench contributions since he was otherwise engaged in discussing the £100m concession on housing benefits announced the following days.

These days, Mr Major is at the centre of most of the Government's politically sensitive activities – negotiating the recent concessions on the community charge rebate and the nurses' pay award, and as a member of the health service review team.

Part of this comes with the job of supervising public spending, but Mr Major has an added interest – as the coming man of the Cabinet.

After four years as a whip and social security minister, when his abilities were recognised mainly by Westminster insiders, in the last few months Mr Major has become a fashionable figure. He has been publicly praised by both Mrs Thatcher and Mr Nigel Lawson, Chancellor of the Exchequer, and has featured in several flattering profiles which have not found anything unfavourable to say about him. He has even been singled out by Mr Norman Tebbit, the new conscience of the Conservative Party, as his type of politician.

Such praise is dangerous for any minister. It attracts envy and criticism. Mr

"Doesn't matter who's in power, I'll still be skint."
Minicab driver

FINANCIAL TIMES

Gordon Brown, Labour's Shadow Chief Secretary, caustically noted in Tuesday's debate that Mr Major had been marked out as the Cabinet's fastest rising star since the Social Services Secretary (the now beleaguered Mr John Moore).

Yet, despite superficial similarities of background with Mr Moore, Mr Major is far from being the new rising hope of the Thatcherites. He is respected by the traditional One Nation Tories as well. Admittedly, his career can be seen as an epitome of the new Britain. Born when his father – a one time trapeze artist and US baseball player – was 66, he grew up in two rooms in Brixton in south London. Leaving school at 16 he worked in an insurance company, as a labourer, was unemployed and then joined Standard Chartered Bank, where he worked closely with Lord Barber, the former Conservative Chancellor. From his teens he was always a Tory, speaking from a local soapbox.

Mr Major stresses the importance of these early experiences yet they have not made him harsh or uncaring. Having seen problems from the other side of the fence, he understands the frustrations and intense dislike of bureaucracy of those at the bottom of the heap.

"I do not care a hoot about the fat cats, the extremely able. What I am concerned about are the chaps who work hard and haven't quite made it – who feel trapped." That is why he backs not only cuts in taxes but also efforts to increase owner-occupation, rented housing and more choice in education.

His outlook is unashamedly meritocratic. He says how much he dislikes the blue/white collar divide. By far the most important advance he sees since 1979, both in the Conservative Party and in the country as a whole, is the increased mobility of opportunity: the meritocrats have replaced the aristocrats.

This puts Mr Major clearly in the post-1979 economic grain, but he recognises the associated social obligations. As a social security minister from 1985 to 1987 he was blooded in rows over cold weather payments and involved in the decisions leading to this month's changes with their greater targeting of benefits. But he escaped most of the criticism associated with this shake-up. He makes no secret that he favours a degree of generosity in defining who should receive help. On other social issues, Mr Major is on the liberal rather than the authoritarian wing of his party – opposed to capital punishment and taking a strong stand on racial issues and against apartheid.

Since entering the Commons for the safe seat of Huntingdon in 1979, he has risen through hard work and astuteness. As a whip, initially under the patronage of Mr John Wakeham, he then impressed Mr Nigel Lawson with his contributions to the daily "morning prayers" meetings at the Treasury and for his highly efficient handling of the finance bill. It was Mr Lawson who sought his appointment as Chief Secretary last June, when he became the first of his Commons intake to enter the Cabinet.

At the Treasury he is highly regarded by civil servants both for his grasp of detail in negotiations and for his ability to sense the political mood – a combination not always seen in a Chief Secretary. Even spending ministers like him for his charm and reasonableness.

Thanks to Mr Lawson and the strong state of public finances, Mr Major has been able to build on the work of his predecessor, Mr John MacGregor, in being able to talk in terms of priorities for increases in certain programmes rather than across the board cuts. But his antennae have been sharp enough to know, generally well in advance, when concessions might be needed.

There was, for instance, no question of resisting full funding of the nurses' pay award.

Mr Major is an aggressive public performer in attacking Labour – to the delight of his own side – though occasionally too much so for the taste of the less partisan. He is also quietly effective on television.

However, Mr Major is sensible enough not to let the current praise go to his head. He understands that this year's fashions do not necessarily last, and he still has some way to go to establish himself as one of the Cabinet heavyweights. Talk of him becoming Chancellor after Mr Lawson is premature. So far he has shown considerable talent as a Westminster and Whitehall operator, but has not developed a broader economic viewpoint – very much Mr Lawson's area.

After another year or so at the Treasury his more likely future is running a big spending department – possibly the environment or health and social security.

Still aged only 45, he has plenty of time on his side and is likely to be at the top of the Conservative Party until well into the next century.

A new way for ministers to set out their claims in the public spending round emerged as John Major confronted the big spenders at the Brighton Tory conference.

MAJOR IN FIGHT FOR £3 BILLION LIMIT ON OVERSPEND

By Philip Webster, Chief Political Correspondent

The Government's bruising public spending battle is reaching a climax in Brighton as the Treasury fights to stop next year's overshoot topping £3 billion and giving the wrong signal to the financial markets about the prospects for inflation.

Mr John Major, the Chief Secretary to the Treasury, yesterday began a series of crunch encounters with the main spending ministers, as details emerged of what appears to be one of the toughest expenditure rounds of the Thatcher Government.

The Times has learnt that for the first time ministers have been held to account for the whole of their budgets, rather than solely being examined on their bids for extra spending over the original allocations. These totalled between £9 billion and £10 billion higher than the £167 billion total of public spending planned for next year.

The Treasury has reluctantly accepted from the outset that some increase over the planned total was inevitable.

But as Mr Major started seeing ministers in his room at the Grand Hotel, it was clear that the Treasury had decided that the excess must not be higher than £3 billion and should be considerably less than that.

There are bound to be serious casualties this week.

Unless there is a surprise cave-in by several key ministers, the "Star Chamber", the arbiter of unsettled disputes, will be called into action at the end of next week.

Mr George Younger, the Secretary of State for Defence, was said by close associates yesterday to be determined to take his case to the "Star Chamber" if necessary.

For the first time, it will be under the chairmanship of Mr Cecil Parkinson, the Secretary of State for Energy and a potential candidate to replace Mr Nigel Lawson as Chancellor.

Mr Parkinson is expected by all ministers to take a hard line if the "Star Chamber" sits.

In a BBC interview last night he said that last year and when the "Star Chamber" had not been required to sit, the threat that it might be convened "terrified into making concessions".

Ministers would be expected to honour the commitment to get expenditure back to the planned totals. The other members chosen so far are Mr Major and Mr John Wakeham, Leader of the Commons. The remainder will be other ministers who settle with Mr Major this week.

The key meetings this week are thought likely to involve Mr Younger, Mr Kenneth Clarke, the Secretary of State for Health, Mr Paul Channon, the Secretary of State for Transport, and Mr Nicholas Ridley, Secretary of State for the Environment.

Mr John Moore, the Secretary of State for Social Security, and Mr Kenneth Baker, the Secretary of State for Education, have still to settle.

Mr Clarke inherited a bid from Mr Moore, his predecessor, which is understood to have been considerably pared down, but he is believed to be meeting resistance to his demands for increased capital investment.

Mr Younger is seeking extra funds for ordering three vessels a year to maintain the surface fleet of 50 frigates and destroyers, and a lively argument is proceeding over which tank will replace the Chieftain at an eventual cost of more than £1 billion.

Mr Baker submitted a bid for extra spending to cover the implementation of the Education Reform Act.

Mr Douglas Hurd, the Home Secretary, whose extra bid included plans for accelerating the prison-building programme and increasing police manpower, is understood to have reached agreement with Mr Major. One of the first budgets to be agreed was Mr Chris Patten's overseas aid allocation.

After several years of rigorous adherence to the planned target, the spending overshoot in the preelection year of 1986 was £4.8 billion.

Last year it was £2.7 billion.

The Treasury believes that if it gets close to, or does not top, last year's excess – effectively cutting the overbids by more than two-thirds – it would be the strongest signal to the markets of how toughly the Government has approached the negotiations.

One of the biggest unresolved arguments has centred on Mr Channon's bid for road-building and maintenance.

Mr Major, interviewed on the BBC, said the round was tough. It was not a question of being mean or generous but of making sure the taxpayer got value for money.

The Tory interest in strong defence was a high card for Defence Secretary George Younger to play in the negotiations.

Younger battles for substantial spending increase

Mr Younger, Defence Secretary, is holding out for a substantial increase in defence spending next year, and is ready to appeal to Mrs Thatcher for support in resisting Whitehall "horse trading" over the cost of the nation's defences.

His stand comes as the Ministry of Defence and the Treasury are reported to be at least £1 billion apart despite intense negotiations between Mr Major, Treasury Chief Secretary, and Mr Younger.

Defence and the question of whether child benefit should be frozen for a second successive year have emerged as the most difficult obstacles to reaching an agreement on next year's spending.

Further negotiations this week are likely to determine whether the "Star Chamber", headed by Mr Parkinson, Energy Secretary, will have to be set up this year to arbitrate between Mr Major and the main spending Ministries.

For the past three years, the Ministry of Defence budget has been virtually static in real terms at around £19 billion.

But this has resulted in intense pressure on the re-equipment budget, and defence chiefs warn that weapons programmes may have to be scrapped if there is no relaxation of the tight spending constraints.

Mr Younger is determined to ensure that the defence budget is set without recourse to the "Star Chamber" and is discussing with Mr Major how the cost of important procurement decisions, such as Trident, the new European fighter aircraft and the new Army tank, can be spread over a number of years. But he insists that it is not an issue which can be the subject of the usual horse trading between the Treasury and Whitehall departments and that the Government must provide the funds necessary to sustain the country's defences.

Ministers believe that Mrs Thatcher is likely to side with Mr Younger because of her insistence on strong defence and her warning to the Tory party conference last week that the West should not relax at the first hopeful sign of change in the Soviet Union.

The negotiations are unlikely to be over when the Commons resumes on Wednesday after the summer recess.

The first business is a two-day defence debate, but the delay in settling the budget means that Mr Younger may not be able to make announcements about several projects, including an air support ship for the Navy.

Meanwhile, Mr Moore, Social Services Secretary, is also at loggerheads with Mr Major over the uprating of child benefit.

The Treasury wants to freeze the benefit as part of a long running campaign to allow it to "wither on the vine".

But Mr Moore, with the backing of a sizable group of Conservative MPs, is pressing for the £7.25 a week benefit to be increased in line with inflation, which would mean an increase of about 40p a week.

Tomorrow, Labour plans to launch an offensive against threatened Government public spending cuts this autumn. It will seek to expose what it claims is the Government's neglect of vitally important services.

Mr Gordon Brown, a Labour Treasury spokesman, said yesterday that those in need should not become the victims of "economic mistakes" by Mr Lawson, the Chancellor.

If child benefit, pensions and other help were hit, it would expose as "hollow and fraudulent" Mrs Thatcher's claim to preside over a generous society.

"Having cut living standards with mortgage rises this summer, the Government now threatens the quality of life in our communities with public spending cuts this autumn.

"Labour will fight any behind-the-scenes Tory deals designed to freeze child benefit, cut income support benefits or impose the £10 eyesight test and £3 dental check up charges.

"Mothers on child benefit or pensioners on income support must not pay the price for the Chancellor's economic mistakes."

John Major's success in completing the 1988 public spending round without recourse to the "Star Chamber" was a key factor in wider recognition for his talents in the party at large. It stood him in good stead when the Prime Minister was considering her next Cabinet reshuffle.

Agreement close on spending curb

By George Jones,
Political Correspondent

The Treasury has resolved its outstanding differences with the main spending ministries and is close to completing one of the toughest expenditure rounds of Mrs Thatcher's Government without recourse to the Cabinet's "Star Chamber".

Mr Major, Treasury Chief Secretary, is now confident of keeping next year's overshoot below £3 billion and demonstrating the Government's determination to keep spending under control at a time of concern over the economy.

The "Star Chamber", headed by Mr Parkinson, Energy Secretary, is likely to meet formally to rubber stamp the settlements between the Treasury and the main spending ministries.

But, for the second year running, Mr Major appears to have succeeded in resolving the arguments without the "Star Chamber" being called in to arbitrate between the Treasury and ministers pressing for increased budgets.

The Treasury's success in averting a series of bruising encounters in the "Star Chamber" is a welcome boost for Mr Lawson, the Chancellor, on the eve of today's Commons economic debate.

Labour intends to launch an attack on the Government's handling of the economy, particularly the recent increase in inflation to the highest level for nearly three years and the prospect of a record trade deficit.

The outcome of the public spending review, to be announced in the autumn economic statement in the first half of next month, has been seen in Westminster and the City as an important indicator of the Government's commitment to tackling rising inflation.

The main loser in the spending review has been Mr Moore, the Social Security Secretary.

He has had to concede the freezing of child benefit for the second year running and is facing an embarrassing Tory back-bench revolt over the new benefit levels which could be announced later this week.

But Mr Moore appears to have suffered a further setback in negotiations with the Treasury over a "face-saving" proposal for help for families to be targeted on the less well-off.

It now looks as if less than the full £130 million cost of uprating child benefit in line with inflation will be switched into the means-tested family credit or income support.

Several Tory MPs issued a warning last night that they were ready to vote against the Government on the issue and Labour is expected to press the Government on child benefit during today's Commons debate.

Mr Robert McCrindle (C, Brentwood) said the freezing of child benefit would create "another poverty trap", while Mr Timothy Raison (C, Aylesbury) said MPs were warning ministers that failing to increase the benefit would be a "great mistake".

Mrs Thatcher, however, is firmly behind the freezing of child benefit as part of a longer term policy of ensuring that it is targeted on less well-off groups, not paid across the board.

However, the Tory manifesto at the election, which promised to continue paying child benefit, is seen as an obstacle to removing it from the better-off.

Mr Channon, the Transport Secretary, has also secured a substantial part of the extra £300 million he has been seeking for increased spending on the roads programme.

DAILY TELEGRAPH

Bus conductor: **"John Major even once applied to the buses but couldn't pass the arithmetic."**

Elderly passenger: **"Oh well ducks, it was pounds, shillings and pence then, wasn't it?"**

Overheard on a number 15 bus

4

Foreign Secretary

If there was a period when Major was seen as uncomfortable as he climbed towards Downing Street, it was his 94 days as Foreign Secretary.

He started the job in an atmosphere of crisis as the press uncovered the messy details behind the Cabinet reshuffle, and the pomp and ceremony of diplomacy were not easy for a man who liked to spend quiet weekends at home in Cambridgeshire and took holidays aboard narrowboats on Britain's canals.

But he set himself to the task willingly and had developed both his knowledge and his experience by the time the next crisis forced the Prime Minister's hand.

Watching cricket gave John Major enormous pleasure, and meeting his heroes was an added bonus for him – if not for the rest of his family!

Replay

Like many cricket fans, Foreign Secretary John Major finds that England's past cricketing glories are a useful way of escaping the dismal performance of the present Test team, as his enthusiasm when he first met Sir Leonard Hutton demonstrates.

Fellow cricketing enthusiast Jeffrey Archer has recalled how, while sitting with Major watching England playing at Lords last year, they saw Hutton in the President of the MCC's box. After much persuasion, Archer introduced the shy Major to meet his hero. Hutton and Major talked happily for the rest of the afternoon.

After meeting Major's son James at a party recently, Archer asked him whether his father had ever mentioned that he had once met the great Yorkshireman.

"Yes," replied James grimly. "Daily."

DAILY TELEGRAPH

"The Cricketing Major."

Thatcher sacks or moves half of the Cabinet: Major marked as heir apparent

The years of backroom work, coaxing, cajoling and occasionally threatening to achieve his targets, and the years of loyalty to his leader, paid off when John Major was appointed to one of the three great offices of state, the Foreign Office.

By GEORGE JONES

MORE than half the members of the Cabinet were either moved or replaced in a series of changes which stunned Tory MPs last night. Mrs Thatcher marked out Mr John Major as her heir apparent by appointing him Foreign Secretary in the most far-reaching Cabinet reshuffle of her ten years in power.

Mr Major, 46, becomes the youngest Foreign Secretary since Dr David Owen 12 years ago, and after only two years in the Cabinet as Treasury Chief Secretary has leapfrogged other senior Ministers to occupy one the most powerful posts in the Government.

Last night Mr Major said he was 'quite astonished' to be offered the post of Foreign Secretary. He had not remotely expected it. Mrs Thatcher has acted decisively to break the log-jam at the top of the Cabinet by appointing Sir Geoffrey Howe, the longest-serving Foreign Secretary since the 1914-18 war, as deputy Prime Minister and Leader of the House of Commons.

The long-awaited reshuffle was designed to bring to the forefront some of the Government's ablest and most forceful communicators in the two key areas of the environment and Europe, where there has been a big mid-term loss of support.

The changes were much bigger than expected. They included the appointment of the Education Secretary, Mr Kenneth Baker, as

DAILY TELEGRAPH

John Moore

All smiles at the Tory Conference

Conservative party chairman.

He is succeeded at Education by Mr John MacGregor, Agriculture Minister.

The embattled Mr Nicholas Ridley has been replaced as Environment Secretary by Mr Chris Patten, and Mr George Younger, Defence Secretary, is a surprise departure.

Four Ministers left the Cabinet. Mr Younger, like Lord Young, the Trade and Industry Secretary, resigned of his own accord to resume a career in business.

But Mr John Moore, the Social Security Secretary, who lost half his department a year ago, and Mr Paul Channon, who has been dogged by disaster at the Department of Transport, were both dropped. Mr Moore is succeeded at Social Security by Mr Tony Newton, Trade and Industry Minister.

The four newcomers into the Cabinet are Mr Patten, who moves from Overseas Development to the Environment Department to raise the Government's profile on green issues; Mr Peter Brooke, the outgoing Conservative party chairman who becomes Northern Ireland Secretary; Mr John Gummer, who takes over as Agriculture Minister; and Mr Norman Lamont, who is promoted within the Treasury to the job of Chief Secretary, responsible for controlling public spending.

Mrs Thatcher took advantage of the voluntary departure of Mr Younger and Lord Young to make sweeping changes and to bring in new faces at some of the most controversial Whitehall departments.

There was a long-awaited move for Mr Tom King, the longest-serving Northern Ireland Secretary, who at the end of the week will succeed Mr Younger as Defence Secretary.

Mr Ridley was switched to the less front-line Department of Trade and Industry. Despite his mauling at the hands of Tory backbenchers over the poll tax and criticism of his attitude over the environment, Mr Ridley remains a valued associate of the Prime Minister, particularly when she has lost two Ministers most closely identified with her, Lord Young and Mr Moore.

Although Mr Cecil Parkinson's move from Energy to Transport was seen by some MPs as a sideways move, Mrs Thatcher made clear to him yesterday that she regarded it as a key post.

Mr Parkinson is replaced at Energy by Mr John Wakeham, who gets a department of his own after more than seven years as 'business manager', first as Chief Whip and then as Leader of the Commons.

Both Mr Lawson, Chancellor of the Exchequer, and Mr Hurd, Home Secretary, are staying put. By keeping Mr Lawson at the Treasury Mrs Thatcher intended to signal the priority she is giving to getting the economy right and bringing inflation down again.

But the most surprising change was the removal of Sir Geoffrey Howe from the Foreign Office, where he has been since 1983.

Sir Geoffrey, who still regards himself as a leadership contender should anything befall Mrs Thatcher, had been resisting a move and until recently, Downing Street had been suggesting there would be no movement in the top three posts.

Sir Geoffrey, according to close colleagues, agreed to move after receiving a number of assurances from Mrs Thatcher: that he would assume the former role of Lord Whitelaw as deputy Prime Minister – even though she said that post was 'unique' and had come to an end when Lord Whitelaw resigned 18 months ago; that he would chair key cabinet committees, including Home Affairs, Legislation and the 'star chamber' which adjudicates in public spending battles; he will have a forward-looking policy role in preparing for the next General Election manifesto.

The move was said to have come as a 'complete surprise' to him. But Sir Geoffrey was said to have agreed to the change of roles out of loyalty to the party and to ensure that the work of the past 10 years was consolidated into a fourth Tory victory at the next election.

Sir Geoffrey will be Lord President of the Council and Leader of the Commons. With his extensive experience of Government, he is expected to assume the mantle of Lord Whitelaw in acting as a steadying influence in the Government and watching out for political 'banana skins'.

His successor, Mr Major, has had the most rapid promotion of any Minister under Mrs Thatcher, and is now clearly seen by her as a possible future leader.

With the appointment of Mr Baker as party chairman, the battle for her succession sometime after the next General Election is now underway.

Mr Major, MP for Huntingdon, was the first member of the 1983 intake to reach the Cabinet. For the past two years he has been in charge of public spending and has impressed Mrs Thatcher and Cabinet colleagues with his tough negotiating skills.

At the Foreign Office, he will be expected to regain the initiative for the Government in Europe in the wake of last month's setback in the European elections, the first Conservative defeat at the hands of the Labour party since 1974.

However, Mr Major may well see the fate of Mr John Moore as a cautionary note. He also had rapid advancement and was talked of as a possible successor to Mrs Thatcher.

But managing the unwieldy Department of Health and Social Security proved too much for Mr Moore, who became ill.

His successor at Social Security, Mr Newton, has been in the Cabinet for a year as deputy to Lord Young at Trade and Industry.

The appointment of Mr Baker as party chairman had been widely expected. But it was a popular move with Tory MPs, who regard him as one of the party's best communicators.

Senior Tories hope his presentational skills will bring new drive and impetus to Conservative Central Office and halt the Tories' mid-term slide in the opinion polls.

He will be joined at Central Office by Lord Young, who has been appointed a deputy party chairman even though he is leaving the Government to resume his business career.

The importance of presentational skills was underlined by the appointment of Mr Chris Patten as Environment Secretary, one of the most controversial posts in the Government. Although a prominent Tory 'wet', Mr Patten has played an important behind the scenes role in the Conservative party, contributing to Mrs Thatcher's speeches and helping to draft the manifesto for the European elections.

At Environment he will be expected to counter the recent surge in support for the Green party as well as improving the Government's showing with the public on environmental issues.

He will also be in charge of introducing the controversial poll tax or community charge in England and Wales next year in the face of a Tory backlash over the proposed 'safety net'.

Westminster was in ferment as details began to emerge of the behind-the-scenes horse-trading before the announcement of the Cabinet reshuffle, with Sir Geoffrey Howe at the centre of the storm.

HOWE REJECTED THATCHER'S OFFER OF HURD'S JOB

Tories fear strain in the Cabinet

By GEORGE JONES, Political Editor

MRS THATCHER'S radical restructuring of the Cabinet was overshadowed last night by controversy over the role of Sir Geoffrey Howe as Deputy Prime Minister and the disclosure that he had been offered and rejected the job of Home Secretary.

As the Prime Minister insisted that the most extensive reshuffle she has carried out would not result in any change of policy, there was concern among Tory MPs that it had strained relations with three of her most senior ministers – Mr Hurd, Home Secretary, Mr Lawson, the Chancellor, and Sir Geoffrey.

It emerged yesterday that Mrs Thatcher had offered Mr Hurd's job to Sir Geoffrey during several hours of negotiations to persuade him to give up the post of Foreign Secretary to make way for Mr John Major.

Mr Hurd, however, was unaware that his job was in the balance and thought he had received earlier assurances from the Prime Minister that she did not propose to move him.

Mr Lawson was asked by Mrs Thatcher to give up his official country residence, Dorneywood in Buckinghamshire, so that it could be an extra inducement to Sir Geoffrey, who was having to hand over the Foreign Secretary's two residences at Carlton House Terrace and Chevening, Kent.

There was also uncertainty at Westminster over the role Sir Geoffrey will perform as Deputy Prime Minister – a post which Mrs Thatcher said 18 months ago was no longer needed.

While Sir Geoffrey was insisting that he would continue to have an important influence on government policies at home and abroad, those close to Mrs Thatcher were describing the role of Deputy Prime Minister as a 'courtesy title' with no constitutional status.

Officials said Sir Geoffrey would chair four important Cabinet committees, but emphasised that Mrs Thatcher would be in charge of the Government even when out of the country.

Mrs Thatcher put the finishing touches to the reshuffle with appointments yesterday to the lower ranks of the Government. Four rising stars on the backbenches join the Government for the first time.

Mr John Redwood, MP for Wokingham, and a former head of the Downing Street Policy Unit, becomes a junior Minister at the Department of Trade and Industry. Mrs Gillian Shephard (Norfolk South-West) becomes Under Secretary for Social Security.

Mr Patrick McLoughlin (Derbyshire, West), a former miner, becomes a junior Transport Minister and Mr David Curry (Skipton and Ripon) becomes Parliamentary Secretary for Agriculture.

Government concern to demonstrate that it was tackling food safety was demonstrated by the designation of one of the new junior Agriculture Ministers,

DAILY TELEGRAPH

Mr David Maclean, as Minister of Food.

Mr Gummer, the new Agriculture Minister, said his ministry would be concerned first and foremost with consumers and would seek to dispel the 'farmers' friend' label given to it by critics.

As 13 Cabinet ministers involved in the reshuffle got used to their new responsibilities, more details emerged of the moving of Sir Geoffrey from the Foreign Office after six years to the less front-line role of Leader of the Commons.

When he was summoned to Downing Street at 8.50 am on Monday, Mrs Thatcher offered him the choice of becoming Home Secretary – the only one of the three principal offices of state he has not yet held – or becoming Leader of the Commons.

Those close to Sir Geoffrey said he was shocked by the Prime Minister's decision, which came 'like a bolt from the blue'.

However, Mrs Thatcher, angered by his insistence that she must change course at the recent Madrid Common Market summit, was determined to remove him from the Foreign Office.

Sir Geoffrey went back to his office, and for a while considered leaving the Government. After consultations with close colleagues, he decided against taking the Home Office.

In telephone talks with Downing Street he sought assurances that the role of Leader of the Commons would include the title and powers of Deputy Prime Minister, last held by Viscount Whitelaw.

Meanwhile, Mr Hurd had no inkling of what was alleged to be going on.

One day last week, in the presence of civil servants, Mrs Thatcher had apparently gone out of her way to confirm, at least provisionally, Mr Hurd in office, saying: 'It's good to see the Home Office so quiet.'

A whole series of international problems faced John Major as he started reading into his new job at the Foreign Office. There was much to do and little time to prepare himself to do it.

Hong Kong challenge for FO's new man

On his first day, John Major meets a president, entertains a prime minister, and comes face-to-face with a world of tough issues

By HELLA PICK, Diplomatic Editor

Within a couple of hours of moving in at the Foreign Office yesterday, Mr John Major, the new Foreign Secretary, was discussing Middle East affairs with President Sheikh Zayed bin Sultan al-Nahyan of the United Arab Emirates.

Soon afterwards Mr Major received a telegram from the Governor of Hong Kong urging him to put a confidence-building visit to the colony high on his agenda.

Last night he was host at a dinner for Mr James Mitchell, Prime Minister, Foreign Minister, and Finance Minister of St Vincent and the Grenadines.

If Sir Geoffrey Howe had still been Foreign Secretary, he would have had talks yesterday afternoon with the Soviet Defence Minister, General Dmitri Yazov. Mr Major decided on a brief postponement, but tomorrow he must be ready to discuss arms control and security issues with the Moscow visitor.

If the 20-nation peace conference on Cambodia begins as scheduled in Paris on Sunday, Mr Major will make his international debut with a speech on South-East Asian affairs. It will be his first opportunity to meet Mr James Baker, the US Secretary of State, and Mr Eduard Shevardnadze, the Soviet Foreign Minister.

A visit to Washington in September is under consideration. In any event Mr Major will be meeting many of his counterparts at the United Nations General Assembly later in September.

These engagements are just a foretaste of the patchwork agenda that awaits the new minister. Unless there is an international crisis he will have most of August, normally a quiet month on the diplomatic front, to read himself into foreign policy issues.

Mr Major has a tough act to follow, if only by virtue of Sir Geoffrey's long experience in foreign affairs, his encyclopaedic knowledge, and the respect he had earned from his foreign counterparts as a negotiator.

The new Foreign Secretary's task is all the harder since all the Foreign Office ministers, except the Minister of State, Mr William Waldegrave, have been replaced by people with little experience of foreign affairs.

This leaves Mrs Thatcher as the most experienced of the ministers handling foreign affairs; and she combines this with an obvious determination to be an important player in international relations.

The world will be watching closely to see whether Mr Major

GUARDIAN

Anglo-French talks at Chequers

becomes his own man, prepared to stand up for his views with greater determination than his predecessor.

He will have no difficulty in identifying his priorities: European Community affairs, especially foreign policy co-ordination among member states; East-West relations, with more and more attention being paid to fostering democracy in Eastern Europe; Middle East questions – the hostages and whether to reopen diplomatic relations with Iran or Syria; the conventional arms and chemical weapons negotiations, where British interests are directly at stake; Southern Africa and the sanctions debate in the run-up to the Commonwealth conference in Kuala Lumpur in October.

Hong Kong poses the most immediate challenge, in terms of both the urgent need to shore up its people's confidence and the looming crisis over the mandatory repatriation of the Vietnamese boat people. Sir Geoffrey prided himself on the Sino-British Joint Declaration, which provides for the transfer of Hong Kong's sovereignty to China in 1997; but his personal stock crashed disastrously when he visited the colony last month.

The Cabinet still has to decide what Britain can do by way of granting right of abode to selected categories people. But it will be the Foreign Secretary's task to convince public opinion in Hong Kong that he is ready to stand up for their interests with China, if necessary arranging an early visit to Beijing, as well as Hong Kong.

With disorder already breaking out in the Vietnamese refugee camps, Mr Major will have to decide quickly whether the repatriation policy can be sustained without bringing misery upon the boat people and international opprobrium upon Britain.

His trip to the Paris summit on Cambodia was John Major's first mission overseas as Foreign Secretary, just six days after he had taken office. His most immediate problem was not Cambodia but Hong Kong and his meeting to discuss the colony with the Chinese Foreign Minister.

Blunt warning from Major over Hongkong

By John Dickie, Diplomatic Editor

JOHN MAJOR dramatically made his mark as Foreign Secretary here yesterday with a blunt warning to China over Hongkong.

Days after succeeding Sir Geoffrey Howe in Mrs Thatcher's Cabinet reshuffle, he told Chinese Foreign Minister Qian Qichen that the people of Hongkong must be reassured their way of life will be preserved.

As the first Western Minister to face Qian Qichen since the massacre of students in Peking, Mr Major surprised everyone with his directness. The unexpected 40 minute confrontation in the British delegation suite at the Paris conference concentrated entirely on the alarm in the colony, which is to be handed over to the Chinese in 1997.

The message: China must act quickly to counter the strength of feeling aroused in Hongkong and Britain by the bloody events of June 3 and 4. He stressed that Hongkong's security and prosperity depended on the restoration of confidence in the future.

Britain has been accused of abandoning the Hongkong people by refusing to grant automatic residence rights to the three million British passport holders.

It had been expected that U.S. Secretary of State James Baker would be first to challenge the Chinese face to face. But Mr Major decided that since Britain and Hongkong had most at stake it was his duty to intervene.

He underlined the need to negotiate parts of the draft Basic Law which will form the constitution of Hongkong as a special administrative region of China after 1997.

Both sides should look again at Article 18, the turmoil clause which has caused fears in Hongkong that, in a state of emergency, troops would be used as they were in Tiananmen Square against the students.

Mr Major emphasised that Hongkong's apprehensions would be overcome only if it were made clear that Chinese troops would be used solely against aggression from outside. There is strong opposition to Chinese troops being stationed in barracks being vacated by the British.

Although Qian Qichen made no specific commitments, the Foreign Secretary hopes to see progress at the resumption of the Joint Liaison Group set up after the Anglo Chinese joint declaration on Hongkong in 1984. Meetings were suspended following the June massacres.

Mr Major lifted the ban and agreed to restart working sessions in London on September 27. A further meeting is expected in Peking before the end of the year.

As he left Qian Qichen, Mr Major said: "We have had some very frank discussions. He is in no doubt about our concern and the need to restore confidence in Hong Kong."

Mr Major steered clear of any commitment to visit Peking. His policy remains one step at a time. But he was forthright in his address to the conference about the need to give Cambodia a fresh start after the killing fields horror of a million deaths under Pol Pot.

DAILY MAIL

Europe was becoming a key issue for the Thatcher Government, and Major was keen to reassure the UK's EC partners on the question of Britain's future within the Community.

MAJOR: I'm no Euro hit man

By John Williams

Mr John Major, the new Foreign Secretary, moved today to reassure Europe that he is not Mrs Thatcher's hit man in a new offensive against Brussels.

After the dismay in the European Community over Sir Geoffrey Howe's removal last week, Mr Major used his first interview on foreign policy to calm fears in European capitals.

Firmly rejecting the idea that his appointment was a sign of hardening British attitudes, he declared that Britain is not "a reluctant member" of the EC.

Mr Major, speaking in Paris, said: "There is no doubt that we have a strong future within the European Community."

The opportunities in the run up to the single market in 1992 would be "immense".

Mr Major's remarks were designed to mollify European hostility aroused by reports that Mrs Thatcher had removed Sir Geoffrey because he was too pro-European.

France's President Mitterrand warned last week that Europe would push ahead with monetary union and other key issues without Britain if necessary.

EVENING STANDARD

Deep concern over Western hostages

Amid deep concern over the fate of Western hostages in Beirut, Mr John Major, the Foreign Secretary, yesterday abandoned his holiday only a day after starting it.

Whitehall was in close contact with Washington and appeared to be coordinating its public statements. President Bush urged all parties holding hostages in the Middle East to release them and end the cycle of violence.

Remarks made by Mr Major yesterday seemed designed to show balance. "Immediately after the capture of Sheikh Obeid, we called urgently for the release of all hostages. President Bush has done the same. The UN Security Council has unanimously demanded the safe release of all hostages wherever, and by whomever, they are being held. We are in touch with a number of countries in the region and with the US Administration. I urge any country with influence to use it to secure the safe return of all hostages," he said.

His reference to "all hostages" was meant to include three Iranians. A Lebanese driver working for them also disappeared in a Christian area in 1982. They are assumed to have been killed by Christian forces, but Iranian authorities have long urged the British to use any influence to find out what became of them.

His statement was much milder than the strong criticism Mr Major made on Monday of the claim by the "Organisation of the Oppressed on Earth" that it had killed Lieutenant-Colonel William Higgins.

The change of tone seemed designed to correct an impression that Britain was tougher on the pro-Iranian group than on the Israelis.

However, other governments continued to make strong statements. Mr Sten Andersson, the Swedish Foreign Minister, said the claimed murder of Colonel Higgins was "a despicable deed".

Iran's newly elected President, Ali Akbar Hashemi Rafsanjani, and Mr Eduard Shevardnadze, the Soviet Foreign Minister, both regretted the killing.

Hojatoleslam Rafsanjani, in his first meeting with a foreign statesman since his election on Friday, also signed a joint statement "condemning all acts of a terroristic nature", Tass, the official Soviet news agency, reported.

Newspapers in Switzerland generally criticised Israel more than the Lebanese militants. Abrar, a leading Tehran paper, defended the claimed execution and accused the West of displaying double standards by condemning it.

The Kuwait Times said: "If Higgins has been hanged, then Israel certainly pulled the rope." Another Kuwaiti daily, Al-Rai Al-Aam, claimed Israel carried out the kidnapping to divert world attention from the intafada.

Syria, which has close links with Amal, the main rival Shia Muslim faction to Hezbollah in Lebanon, deplored the colonel's death and, with Jordan and the PLO, denounced Israel's abduction of the Muslim cleric as a "terrorist" act.

Mr Boutros Boutros Ghali, Minister of State for Foreign Affairs of Egypt, the only Arab state with a peace treaty with Israel, told reporters that, while Egypt expressed deep sorrow and condemnation for the killing of Higgins, "this does not lessen what Israel has done in acts of violence which Egypt has already said will lead to more acts of violence".

THE TIMES

The thorny issue of South Africa was the most contentious on the agenda at the Commonwealth heads of government meeting in Kuala Lumpur, and the actions of the British leader aroused considerable anger. Also, there were reports that the issue had caused a damaging rift between Mrs Thatcher and Mr Major.

Thatcher hits back at irate Commonwealth leaders

From Robin Oakley, Political Editor, Kuala Lumpur

Commonwealth leaders reacted furiously yesterday to Mrs Thatcher's tactics in distancing herself from the Kuala Lumpur declaration on South Africa. But she hit back, virtually accusing the rest of the Commonwealth of seeking to deny her the right of free speech.

Mr Robert Mugabe, the President of Zimbabwe, said that Mrs Thatcher and Mr John Major, the Foreign Secretary, by issuing a separate communique spelling out in detail Britain's objections to four paragraphs in the Commonwealth declaration, had done something "despicable and unacceptable". He accused Mrs Thatcher of torpedoing the Commonwealth declaration to signal to South Africa that Britain supported apartheid. Mr Mugabe added: "I'm sure Britain is doing it merely because she feels she is the Commonwealth, which she is not."

Other Commonwealth heads of government viewed the British action as a deliberate attempt to lessen the impact of the official declaration and as discourteous because they were given no prior warning.

The other leaders believed they had made concessions on the basis of an apparent British movement towards consensus on sanctions policy, only to find Mrs Thatcher dissociating herself from the deal thrashed out by Mr Major and other foreign ministers. Mr Brian Mulroney, the Canadian Prime Minister, was described by aides as so angry that he was "ropeable".

When Dr Mahathir Mohamed, the Malaysian Prime Minister and conference chairman, opened the official proceedings in private yesterday Mr Mulroney called for an explanation from Mrs Thatcher, saying that other countries had had to "water their wine" in achieving the conference declaration.

He said: "When you sign a document at five you don't repudiate it at six." The price of membership of the Commonwealth, he said, was loyalty and fairness, implying that Mrs Thatcher had displayed neither. Mr Bob Hawke, the Australian Prime Minister, also accused Mrs Thatcher of repudiating the official communique, declaring: "This is not the way things should be done."

But Mrs Thatcher hit back. "I don't think any explanation is called for," she said. "I am astounded that anyone should object."

British sources expressed amazement that the Commonwealth "should find free speech so inconvenient". They said Britain had been prevented from spelling out in the official communique why it had refused to endorse four photographs and that Mrs Thatcher was appalled that any member of the Commonwealth should object to her setting out the reasons for her reservations.

Britain's four reservations were in refusing to accept that sanctions had affected Pretoria's policies or to agree to tighten sanctions, and in opposing the setting up of an agency to monitor South Africa's international financial links and the maintenance of the Commonwealth Committee of Foreign Ministers to watch over sanctions policies.

The recriminations completely overshadowed the official business of the latest memorandum on debt, drugs and other issues. The conference winds up today with the issue of the final communique and press conferences by the leaders.

As Mr Major flew home yesterday Downing Street sources swiftly dismissed rumours of a rift between him and Mrs Thatcher. The Foreign Secretary had always been due to fly home early to be back in time for his first session of Foreign Office questions in the commons.

The rift stories arose because Mr Major appeared visibly shocked when first told by a radio interviewer that official spokesmen had announced Mrs Thatcher's dislike of the document which he had negotiated with the committee of Foreign Ministers.

Mr Major's claim on Sunday night that the others in the Commonwealth had been "dragged towards" Britain's view seemed to sit a little uncomfortably with the acknowledgement by British sources that the Prime Minister "did not much like" the official document.

It was explained yesterday that Mrs Thatcher thought her Foreign Secretary had done "a damned good job" in protecting British interests and had achieved all that could have been hoped for.

LONDON: Labour last night accused Mrs Thatcher of "double-dealing" Mr Major in the sanctions row as suspicion mounted among the Opposition that the two are at loggerheads.

Mr Neil Kinnock said: "Mrs Thatcher is double-dealing the Commonwealth and double-dealing her own Foreign Secretary."

The applause continues for the Foreign Secretary's speech to the Tory party conference in 1989.

Major issues denial of policy rift

By Jon Lewis, Political Staff

"Who is this nice man who has risen to the top without bloodletting, without revealing himself? Is he right, left or centre?"

Le Figaro, French daily newspaper

Mr John Major, the Foreign Secretary, went to the extraordinary length last night of issuing a detailed denial of a damaging rift between himself and the Prime Minister over the statement they made at the Commonwealth conference in Kuala Lumpur qualifying Britain's position on South Africa.

The Foreign Secretary, who returned from Malaysia early yesterday, was clearly anxious to limit the damage from press reports of the split. He said from his Huntingdon home that the stories "utterly misrepresent the position".

Reports of the differences caused deep disquiet among Conservative MPs. They believe the Prime Minister had let down her Foreign Secretary, treating him as her puppet by issuing the qualifying statement and detracting from the success she and Mr Major had had in persuading the Commonwealth not to increase sanctions.

In interviews in Kuala Lumpur, Mrs Thatcher also dismissed rumours of a rift as "absolute poppycock". She said Mr Major is "absolutely outstanding as a negotiator, extremely clear in everything he says, and respected by all".

Mr Major said: "There is and has been no disagreement between the Prime Minister and me over either the communique or our draft statement. In the communique negotiated with other foreign ministers, there were four areas where I declined to accept their views.

"The communique states this clearly. The Prime Minister agreed with my reservations and accepted the communique without alteration.

"We decided, however, to issue a joint statement to explain our policy on those areas where we disagreed with colleagues. Had we not done so, their views would have been known on these matters, but ours would not. That would clearly have been unacceptable. I am surprised that anyone takes the view that the Commonwealth can set out its view, but Britain should not." When Sir Geoffrey Howe, the Deputy Prime Minister, answered questions for Mrs Thatcher in the Commons yesterday – himself the subject of reported differences with the Prime Minister when he was Foreign Secretary – he insisted Mr Major had been consulted on "each of the steps".

The draft communique and the subsequent statement were agreed by telephone as the Foreign Secretary and the Prime Minister were fulfilling different engagements.

Whether Mr Major's reassurance will end Conservative backbench apprehension was still open to doubt last night. Some Conservative MPs on the left of the party claimed that MPs and their constituency parties were "seething".

Mr Peter Temple-Morris, the vice-chairman of the Conservative backbench foreign affairs committee, declared last night: "The essential decision was whether or not to sign the agreement which had been well negotiated by John Major. Having taken the decision to sign and been applauded for it, it would have been far better if one had kept the dignity of silence." Mr Alan Beith, the Liberal Democrat Treasury spokesman, said: "Whether she is in Kuala Lumpur dealing with foreign policy or in Downing Street dealing with the economy, the Prime Minister cannot resist destroying the credibility of her ministers."

THE TIMES

Reading the lesson at a memorial service for the mother of Beirut hostage John McCarthy

Problems were mounting for Mrs Thatcher.

Walters gagged as Lawson wins

By GEORGE JONES, Political Editor

MRS THATCHER intervened yesterday to avert a new rift with Mr Lawson, Chancellor of the Exchequer, by agreeing to his demand that her economic adviser, Sir Alan Walters, should not make public comments about government policy.

Sir Alan, who is due to return to Downing Street from Washington in 10 days' time, is to be reminded by the Cabinet Office that he is bound by the rules of confidentiality which apply to civil servants.

One of Mrs Thatcher's first engagements after returning from the Kuala Lumpur summit in the early hours of yesterday was a 45-minute meeting with Mr Lawson on the economy.

Although officials refused to disclose what had been discussed, it emerged afterwards that Mrs Thatcher had accepted Mr Lawson's unprecedented demand that Sir Alan should be silenced.

But she is resisting demands from Tory MPs that Sir Alan should be sacked for undermining the Chancellor's authority with his comment that the European Monetary System is 'half-baked'.

Government officials went out of their way to defend Sir Alan, pointing out that the offending article – in which he said Mrs Thatcher 'concurred' with his view on the EMS – had been written in the middle of last year before he was reappointed as a part-time adviser to Mrs Thatcher.

But Mr Lawson appears to have emerged the victor from a remarkable bout of Whitehall infighting, which has alarmed Conservative MPs and ministers and brought renewed criticism of the Prime Minister's style of government.

In the Commons yesterday, Tory MPs demonstrated their support for another senior minister, Mr Major, the Foreign Secretary, who again denied reports that he had been at odds with Mrs Thatcher over South African sanctions at the Commonwealth summit.

Mr Major rejected Labour allegations that Mrs Thatcher had repudiated the agreement he had negotiated with other Commonwealth foreign ministers.

But, when Mr Gerald Kaufman, Labour's foreign affairs spokesman, urged him to follow Mr Lawson's example and stand up against the Prime Minister's advisers, Mr Major declared: 'As Foreign Secretary, I will make up my own mind as I was appointed to do.' Mrs Thatcher is likely to face questioning from MPs today when she makes her first appearance in the Commons since returning from Kuala Lumpur. She will be answering Prime Minister's questions and making a statement on the Commonwealth summit.

Mr Kinnock, Labour leader, made clear last night that he does not regard the Walters affair as closed. In a speech on

DAILY TELEGRAPH

the economy, he described Sir Alan as a 'newly-ordained Trappist monk'.

It was Labour goading on Sir Alan's views during a Commons debate on the economy that prompted Mr Lawson to issue his demand for Mrs Thatcher to remind Sir Alan that he was bound by Civil Service rules not to make public the advice he has given to Ministers.

Mr Lawson is said by colleagues to be furious at the way Sir Alan has taken issue with his economic policies.

He has been supported by the influential 1922 Committee of Tory backbenchers in demanding that Sir Alan should be instructed to keep quiet and stop undermining Government efforts to present a united front on the economy.

In a further attempt to mollify the Chancellor, Government officials also distanced themselves from Sir Alan's statement that Mrs Thatcher had so far concurred with his view that Britain should stay out of the exchange rate mechanism.

It was stated authoritatively that this was not the stance of the Government. The Prime Minister, it was said, stood by her commitment at the Madrid EEC summit in June that Britain would become a full member of the EMS as soon as certain conditions had been met.

5

Chancellor

Mrs Thatcher's options were narrowing when Nigel Lawson dramatically quit. There was talk in the air of her succession, the inevitable first step towards her departure, although there was no hint of the dramatic events to follow just 13 months later.

In the wings, Michael Heseltine was already waiting for his chance to strike towards the leadership, and John Major inherited huge problems from his predecessor as the economy was starting to drift towards recession.

There was no doubt, however, that the promotion was a homecoming for Major, back to facts and figures from a world of less tangible realities.

The undercurrent of turmoil that had dogged the Prime Minister for some weeks surfaced with the resignation of Nigel Lawson, then refused to go away. With hindsight, some commentators said he got out just in time, before the decisions he had taken on interest rates in the preceding months came home to roost – producing big problems for his successor, John Major.

The dramatic resignation badly wounded the Prime Minister, but characteristically she bounced off the ropes with her customary determination, speed and vigour to announce within a few minutes her restructured Cabinet, which brought John Major back to managing the economy.

It was the end of a comparatively uneasy three months in the Foreign Office, where the issues were so large and complex that even the workaholic Major had only just been starting to gain confidence.

Crisis for Thatcher after Lawson quits as Chancellor:

Major is moved to No 11: Hurd for Foreign Office

By GEORGE JONES

NIGEL LAWSON stunned the political world and plunged Mrs Thatcher into her biggest crisis as Prime Minister by resigning as Chancellor of the Exchequer last night in protest at the continued presence of Sir Alan Walters as her personal economic adviser. Mr Lawson's simmering discontent over the way his economic policies had been 'second guessed' in No 10 Downing Street by Sir Alan finally boiled over into the most sensational Ministerial resignation since Mr Michael Heseltine walked out of the Cabinet over Westland in January 1976.

In a night of dramatic developments at Westminster, Sir Alan – who is in Washington – also quit as Mrs Thatcher's economic adviser. After hearing of Mr Lawson's resignation, he telephoned the Prime Minister to say it would be best for him to 'step aside'.

Mrs Thatcher moved quickly to steady a badly shaken Government and Conservative party by appointing Mr John Major, the Foreign Secretary, as Chancellor. Mr Douglas Hurd, Home Secretary for the past four years, was promoted to the Foreign Office, while the Government Chief Whip, Mr David Waddington, became Home Secretary. Both men were cheered by Tory MPs when they appeared in the Commons last night, and the appointments were clearly designed to steady Tory morale.

It is a meteoric rise for Mr Major, 46, a former Treasury Minister, who has been Foreign Secretary for just three months.

But there was no doubt at Westminster last night that Mr Lawson's resignation was a body blow personally for Mrs Thatcher and the Government as a whole.

Shocked Tory MPs and Ministers said they feared it could destabilise the Government as well as triggering an economic crisis at a time when confidence in the economy has been shaken by high interest rates and a record trade deficit. Opposition MPs claimed the Government was in a shambles, and the Commons was forced to adjourn temporarily in confusion when Mr Lawson's resignation was announced.

As Tory MPs filed out of the chamber in a state of disbelief and amazement, a group of jubilant Labour MPs began singing the Red Flag. In a terse letter of resignation, Mr Lawson told the Prime Minister he could no longer serve as Chancellor while Sir Alan – who has publicly criticised his policies, particularly support for full British membership of the European Monetary System – continued to advise her. 'The successful conduct of economic policy is possible only if there is, and is seen to be, full agreement between the Prime Minister and the Chancellor of the Exchequer.

'Recent events have confirmed that this essential requirement

DAILY TELEGRAPH

Nigel Lawson and his wife, Therese, after his resignation.

cannot be satisfied so long as Alan Walters remains your personal economic adviser.

'I have therefore regretfully concluded that it is in the best interests of the Government for me to resign my office without further ado,' said Mr Lawson.

In three meetings with Mr Lawson in her Downing Street study yesterday, Mrs Thatcher tried in vain to persuade him to stay. Officials said she was 'shocked and sad' at his decision. But she was not prepared to accept the one condition which would have made Mr Lawson reconsider his decision to quit: that she should sack Sir Alan.

In Washington last night a secretary speaking for Sir Alan said he did not wish to make any public comment about his own resignation and Mr Lawson's departure.

Mrs Thatcher first learned of the possibility that Mr Lawson was considering resignation at a meeting with him shortly before 9am yesterday, when they discussed how she would reply to the inevitable questions about Sir Alan during Prime Minister's question time.

Later, at the weekly Cabinet meeting, Mr Lawson was unusually quiet and neither economic issues nor the role of Sir Alan were discussed. Other Cabinet Ministers had no idea then that he was about to resign – though several commented afterwards that he had not been 'his usual ebullient self'.

Just before 2.30pm, as Mrs Thatcher was preparing for questions and her Commons statement on the Commonwealth summit, Mr Lawson walked through the connecting door between No 11 and No 10 Downing Street for a further meeting with the Prime Minister.

He told her of his intention to resign, but she asked him to hold off until they could discuss the matter after her appearance in the Commons. She had a gruelling 75-minute Commons session, in which Mr Kinnock, the Labour leader, taunted her about her 'two Chancellors' – Mr Lawson and Sir Alan – and challenged her to state which of the two she supported.

Despite knowing that when she returned to Downing Street she could be facing a major crisis, Mrs Thatcher gave a robust performance. At one point she labelled Mr Kinnock as 'plumb stupid' for accusing her of speaking with a 'forked tongue' at the Commonwealth summit.

During the question-time exchanges, Mrs Thatcher signalled her support for both Sir Alan and Mr Lawson, saying it was for 'advisers to advise and Ministers to decide'. She said she had 'always supported the Chancellor and his handling of the economy'.

Mr Lawson, however, was absent from the Commons front bench during these exchanges, and when Mrs Thatcher returned to Downing Street shortly after 4.30pm, he tendered his resignation. An hour later she saw Mr Major and offered him the job of Chancellor.

Officials said the Government's economic and monetary policies remained unchanged.

In her reply to Mr Lawson's resignation letter, Mrs Thatcher spoke of her 'profound regret' at his decision, since 'it was my earnest hope that you would continue your outstanding stewardship as Chancellor of the Exchequer for at least the rest of this Parliament'.

Mrs Thatcher insisted there was no difference in their basic economic beliefs, and said the Cabinet would miss the 'great ability and breadth of understanding' which he had brought to their deliberations.

Close colleagues of Mr Lawson said last night that while his discontent over Sir Alan had been simmering for some time, there had not been a personal clash between him and Mrs Thatcher.

He warned her last summer, when she reappointed Sir Alan as her personal economic adviser, that it could lead to trouble. The last straw was Sir Alan's article for an American magazine in which he described the European Monetary System, which Mr Lawson supports, as 'halfbaked' and claimed that Mrs Thatcher concurred with his view.

That reopened the whole issue of who decided economic policy: the Chancellor in No 11 Downing Street or Sir Alan and the Prime Minister next door in No 10.

Mr Lawson felt the continuing speculation, in the press and in the City, made his position untenable and was creating uncertainty which was undermining the Government and the economy.

'He came to the conclusion that the most dignified and honourable thing to do was to go,' said one close friend. 'He was very calm and dignified. There was no row.' Apparently Mr Lawson will not be giving any press conferences or interviews. 'He is trying to make a dignified exit,' said colleagues.

For the immediate future, he will remain an MP but he is expected to seek a City post.

The news of his sudden resignation stunned Tory MPs. Sir William Clark, chairman of the party's backbench finance committee, described it as 'shocking news'.

'It is serious for the Government, and it is bound to have implications for sterling and the stockmarket,' said Sir William.

Mr Kinnock described it as a 'devastating blow to the Prime Minister', while in the Commons Mr Frank Dobson, one of Labour's front bench spokesmen, protested at the way the 'great offices of state' were being passed around like a 'cast-off old coat'.

In private, senior Tory MPs were critical of Mrs Thatcher for allowing relations between her and the Chancellor to deteriorate to such a pitch that he felt he had to resign.

There is little love for Sir Alan among Tory backbenchers or

Doing his bit for charity: Nigel Lawson after his resignation.

Ministers, who have been angered by his public criticisms of the Chancellor's policies. Several said last night that Mrs Thatcher should have sacked Sir Alan if that was the price to keep Mr Lawson on board.

Mr Lawson's sudden departure also raised questions about Mrs Thatcher's style of government, which Ministers and MPs have complained is increasingly autocratic. 'First Michael Heseltine walked out. Then she had to move Sir Geoffrey Howe from the Foreign Office because she could not get on with him. Now we lose the Chancellor. There must be something wrong,' said one senior Tory.

There is little doubt that Mrs Thatcher will face considerable discontent among her MPs over the loss of Mr Lawson.

Although Sir Alan has quit of his own accord, there will also be calls for her to reduce the influence of her own advisers in Downing Street, not least her principal private secretary, Mr Charles Powell, who has already been dubbed the 'alternative Foreign Secretary'.

Many Tories were also angry that Mrs Thatcher had allowed Sir Alan to 'second guess' the Chancellor for so long, effectively denying him the freedom to manage the economy in the way he wanted to do. That, they said, was a fundamental misjudgment and one which could have longer term implications for Mrs Thatcher.

Mr Lawson's resignation is undoubtedly the biggest crisis Mrs Thatcher has faced since becoming Prime Minister 10 years ago. It could well prove more serious than both the Falklands and the Westland affair, because of the economic implications.

With the pound under pressure, and the economy on the brink of recession, the uncertainty caused by Mr Lawson's departure could cause a deepening crisis which undermines the Government's confidence.

Unless the crisis blows over quickly, then the possibility of a challenge to her leadership may well be canvassed within the party at Westminster.

But the speed with which Mrs Thatcher moved to reshape her Government – and the men she has chosen to fill the gaps created by Mr Lawson's departure – did much to steady party morale.

Mr Major is a rising star, widely liked among Tory MPs, and is seen as a possible successor to Mrs Thatcher.

Mr Hurd is regarded as one of the most successful Home Secretaries since Mrs Thatcher has been Prime Minister and as a former Foreign Office official has been seen as a natural Foreign Secretary for some time.

Mr Waddington, a former Home Office Minister, has been a successful chief whip during a time when tensions have been rising within the party and the Government. In a statement last night, Mr Major said he was sorry Mr Lawson had resigned, and he had been proud to serve under him at the Treasury as Chief Secretary. But he made clear the Lawson policies of high interest rates to combat inflation would continue. 'Inflation is the most damaging problem we face and its defeat remains our overriding objective. Monetary policy is tight and is beginning to have its effect. I shall keep it as tight for as long as necessary.' said Mr Major. 'There is no doubt about the underlying strength of the economy. It is better managed, more productive and more efficient than it has ever been.

'Investment is running at a record level. Our export performance is strong. I intend to sustain this improvement in the economy while maintaining existing policies to deal with inflation.'

A CHANCE FOR THE POODLE TO BARK AND BITE

A successor who will have to be even bolder

IAN AITKEN

IT IS a fair bet that John Major, one of the shortest-serving Foreign Secretaries on record, could have done without the promotion he suddenly got just after six o'clock last night. To be Mrs Thatcher's lap dog in foreign affairs is bad enough. To become her poodle in economic policy is much worse.

It has long been one of the most extraordinary features of Mrs Thatcher's Cabinet that there have been so many grown-up politicians willing to put up with almost anything to retain office. Mr Lawson is one of the very few members of her Government who have always shown signs of independence. He demonstrated last night that, like Michael Heseltine, he was willing to stand up to the Iron Lady even to the point of walking out.

But what is one to make of the man who cheerfully takes over in such circumstances, knowing that the issue at stake in the resignation of his predecessor was whether he or the Prime Minister's part-time adviser was running the economy? Mr Major is not, on the face of it, an obvious political weakling. He has had a reasonable run round the Whitehall departments, including a valuable stint as Chief Secretary to the Treasury before his astonishing projection into the Foreign Secretaryship. Moreover, he has done his turn in what is still laughingly known in Whitehall as a 'caring' ministry when he served as Minister for Social Security at the old DHSS before the 1987 General Election.

It was that General Election which put Mr Major on a sharply upward path. He distinguished himself right under the eyes of Herself during several Conservative election press conferences. His confidence under fire, and his grasp of complex statistical questions to do with social security benefits, visibly pleased the Prime Minister.

But although he was tagged by reporters then as a man who was likely to obtain preferment, few people at Westminster were ready for the extraordinary development last July when Mrs Thatcher effectively sacked Sir Geoffrey Howe as Foreign Secretary and replaced him with the still relatively unknown Mr Major. It was a stunning move, and it instantly raised doubts about Mrs T's continuing grasp of political reality.

Had Sir Geoffrey stood his ground and shown himself as ready as Mr Lawson to sacrifice office, then it is quite possible that he would still be Foreign Secretary and might quite conceivably be Deputy Prime Minister as well. As it turned out, he knuckled under and allowed Mr Major to pole vault into one of the key offices of state.

There was real doubt at the

GUARDIAN

time whether this extraordinary move did not imply paranoia on the Prime Minister's part. No one doubted that it arose directly from the obvious disagreements between Howe and Thatcher over the EEC and the European Monetary System in Madrid, when Howe managed to finesse her into some form of deal with her summit partners.

But the ultimate demonstration of Mrs Thatcher's determination to run a one-woman show came last weekend in Kuala Lumpur, when she rode straight over her Foreign Office advisers to display, almost as a matter of principle, her total isolation from the other 48 members of the Commonwealth. If Mr Major did anything much to cool her down, it was not obvious to many of those present.

In his bumbling way, Sir Geoffrey Howe would at least have made the attempt to hose her down and placate the more senior members of the Commonwealth.

But Mr Major must have known that he got the job largely because he wouldn't attempt the same sort of thing. Few people took seriously the story of a 'rift' between him and the Prime Minister.

The experience of Kuala Lumpur does not hold out much hope that Chancellor Major will behave very differently over economic policy than Foreign Secretary Major behaved over South African sanctions. Even with Professor Walters now on the casualty list from yesterday's Whitehall earthquake, it seems probable that Mr Major will be a Walters Chancellor.

Or will he? If the events of the past 24 hours mean anything, they must surely mean that Mrs Thatcher's days at 10 Downing Street really are numbered. And if they are, wouldn't it be a good idea for a new Chancellor to demonstrate that he isn't just a wounded premier's poodle? The reality last night was that, all of a sudden, the Whitehall logjam created by 10 years of Thatcherite hegemony is at last beginning to move. Mr Major is too shrewd a man to miss the chance that development offers. After all, he is the son of a high-wire artist.

Whatever else happens, it will never be glad confident morning again for Mrs Thatcher. When she finally gathers her new and radically reshuffled Cabinet around her next week there will surely be one or two among them who have the courage to say: 'Margaret, this can't go on.' There will be some real changes this time.

There was hope of a positive side to the crisis, and of a change of direction in the tide of Tory affairs.

A CRISIS, AND AN OPPORTUNITY

THE RESIGNATION of Mr Nigel Lawson has created the most serious crisis of Mrs Thatcher's administration since the Falklands War, perhaps even since 1979. Her Government has suffered its moments of dissension and embarrassment, but never a resignation or a sacking that caused such turmoil. The abrupt manner of the Chancellor's going is a grievous blow to Conservative morale. If his difference with Sir Alan Walters was the last straw, it seems a reflection of a wider malaise in the conduct of Cabinet business. The Chancellor, of all people, was being asked to conduct his high-wire act of getting inflation down – for which the confidence of speculators mattered as much as his own – under extraordinary handicaps, when he knew that his policies were being undermined by court favourites at No 10 Downing Street.

Yet, at moments of crisis, the Prime Minister's personal courage and determination are seen to advantage. She has moved swiftly to appoint Mr John Major to succeed the Chancellor. His qualifications for this office are, in many respects, more obvious than those he possessed for the Foreign Secretaryship. He was an outstanding Treasury Chief Secretary, and he is also a more natural and gregarious political animal than his predecessor. He is well placed to preserve party confidence and unity at a period of economic uncertainty. Mr Douglas Hurd possesses outstanding qualifications for the Foreign Secretaryship. However unfortunate the circumstances in which he succeeds to the office, it represents a just reward for his arduous years at the Home Office. Mr David Waddington is a former Home Office Minister with the toughness and ability to make a worthy Secretary of State.

All the Prime Minister's new appointments thus far, then, seem sensible. It is also possible to perceive some consolations in the Chancellor's departure. The air has finally been cleared. There was no prospect of Mr Lawson continuing in office until the next election. He had no obvious further Cabinet ambition. His departure was thus a matter of timing. There was a case for maintaining continuity as the pressures in the economy mounted. But, against that, the declarations of confidence between the Chancellor and the Prime Minister were becoming more forced and less convincing to the markets – or, indeed, to the man in the street – with every passing day. Nor could it be denied that Mr Lawson's own reputation was declining, as economic difficulties grew.

If any good is to come of this affair, the change in the Chancellorship must be accompanied by a demonstrative reversion to Cabinet government. If Mr Major is perceived as a mere political factotum, the results for himself, for international confidence and, in the longer term, for the Prime Minister,

DAILY TELEGRAPH

will be sombre indeed. To that extent, Mr Lawson's resignation may mark a watershed in the fortunes of this Conservative administration. What is being asked of the Prime Minister is something that it is most difficult for her to concede. She has shown political adaptability on many occasions; now she must demonstrate a sincere change of style in the management of government. Leadership, in which she excels, must not degenerate into dominance, intolerance and a simple refusal to work with those she has appointed to serve her. Even before the Lawson decision, there was mounting evidence in the country of a certain restlessness with her style. Many Tory MPs have displayed instinctive sympathy for Mr Lawson in recent days. If the appropriate lessons about presidential government have not been learned from this melodrama, then the price at the polls may eventually prove high indeed.

Finally, it would be wrong to allow the former Chancellor to depart without some words of gratitude. In the spring of 1988, a serious miscalculation about interest rates pre- cipitated economic difficulties which he has since been struggling to correct. But in his earlier years in office, Mr Lawson made a great contribution to this reforming Conservative Government. His sweeping tax cuts and reforms, his prudent management of the public finances, provided an inspiration. His style, his immense intellectual power, justified even the arrogance which so irritated some of his colleagues. He deserves to be remembered by his party and the country for his years of triumph, rather than for the manner of his eclipse.

"If Mr Major is perceived as a mere political factotum, the results for himself, for international confidence and, in the longer term, for the Prime Minister, will be sombre indeed."

The markets were highly volatile in the aftermath of Lawson's resignation, but caution was the order of the day as John Major sought to calm the storm of speculation.

Cautious Major shores up pound to steady sterling

By Sheila Gunn, Political Reporter

Mr John Major's instinct for caution helped him to survive his first day as Chancellor of the Exchequer without the indignity of being forced to raise interest rates.

In his first key decision on entering the Treasury, he ordered the Bank of England to use Britain's currency reserves to shore up the pound.

The move gave him essential breathing space against the prospect of a sterling crisis for, although share prices tumbled, the pound steadied.

However, Mr Major refused to respond to MPs who demanded an immediate Commons statement on future economic policy.

Instead, after a 94-day break away from the Treasury, he returned quietly soon after dawn to spend the day in his new Whitehall office monitoring reaction on the world markets to the shock resignation of his predecessor and former superior, Mr Nigel Lawson.

Apart from a short, official audience with the Queen yesterday afternoon, he did not leave the Treasury, taking a working lunch with officials.

Although he issued no statement and refused to give in-depth interviews in his first full day in office, the Chancellor finished the day with a speech to Conservatives at Northampton warning them that there is a 'difficult period ahead'. MPs and the City will expect him to spell out in more detail in the near future his stance on controlling inflationary pressures.

He must also lay to rest the thorny question of Britain's entry into the Exchange Rate Mechanism of the European Monetary System which came to symbolise the rift between Mr Lawson and Sir Alan Walters, Mrs Thatcher's former economic adviser.

Sources close to Mr Major denied that the new Chancellor had demanded Sir Alan's resignation before accepting the post. The timing of his appointment rules out such an agreement, they say.

Mr Major announced within minutes of his appointment that he intended to maintain Mr Lawson's economic policies, implying the use of high interest rates to control money supply. He said: "Monetary policy is tight and is beginning to have its effect. I shall keep it tight for as long as necessary."

So far he has refused to expand on the statement. He had agreed to be interviewed on BBC Radio 4's The World at One programme, but bowed out and kept his silence.

With some prescience, Mr Major said in July: "Quick reactions in economic policy

DAILY TELEGRAPH

are almost invariably wrong. Once you settle on an economic policy, you should stay with what you've settled on." In making a plea for a "radical" Conservative Party at a fringe meeting in Blackpool this month, he said the real test of the Government's nerve came with its strategy to restore sound money. "To stick to that strategy in the face of steadily rising unemployment and the political pressures which that rise generated must go down as one of the more remarkable feats of any Government in a democracy." In Mr Major's favour is his high reputation among Treasury officials, many of whom describe him as the best Chief Secretary they have had.

It was his success in managing two tough public spending rounds while still maintaining good personal relations with his Cabinet colleagues, together with his right-wing credentials, which led Mrs Thatcher to propel him up the Cabinet ladder to become Foreign Secretary in July.

However, his three-month absence from the Treasury finished on a sour note when he was accused of being Mrs Thatcher's "poodle" at the Commonwealth conference in Kuala Lumpur.

Mr Major caused further dismay this week when in his first – and last – foreign question time in the Commons, he disclosed he might be willing to sanction the forcible repatriation of up to 40,000 Vietnamese boat people from Hong Kong.

Although he issued no statement and refused to give in-depth interviews in his first full day in office, the Chancellor finished the day with a speech to Conservatives at Northampton warning them that there is a 'difficult period ahead'.

Lawson right to quit: poll

A MAJORITY of voters believe Nigel Lawson was right to quit as chancellor of the exchequer last Thursday, according to an opinion poll conducted for The Sunday Times by Market & Opinion Research International (Mori).

The poll shows 55% think Lawson made the right decision in returning to the backbenches, though the verdict on his six years as chancellor is mixed, with 35% satisfied with his performance and 44% dissatisfied.

Among Tory supporters, however, the Lawson years are viewed in a much more positive light, with nearly two thirds satisfied and 21% dissatisfied. Only 47% felt he was right to quit.

But the dramatic events have not worsened the government's standing. A telephone survey conducted after Lawson's resignation, and ending yesterday afternoon, shows the Tories doing rather better than they fared in Mori's regular monthly survey which was held before the resignation.

The regular poll puts the state of the parties at Labour 48% (the same as last month), Tories 38% (five points down), Liberal Democrats 5% (one point down), Greens 5% (two points down), SDP 3% (no change) and others 1%.

The later telephone survey gives Labour at 46% and Conservatives at 39%, a better result for the Tories. But, allowing for normal sampling error, polling by telephone and the smaller sample involved, both polls are roughly consistent with each other.

The Lawson resignation made a big public impact, with 97% of those questioned aware it had taken place; 86% had heard the news by Thursday night. Three-quarters heard the details on television.

Encouragingly for John Major the chancellor, just over half of those questioned spontaneously identified him as Lawson's successor, a breakthrough for one of the cabinet's less well-known faces.

But Major's 13-week career as foreign secretary has made little public impact, with only 17% satisfied with his performance, 9% dissatisfied and the rest having no opinion.

Nearly half those questioned identified Douglas Hurd as Major's successor at the Foreign Office.

Technical note: Mori's subsidiary, On-Line Telephone Surveys Ltd, conducted 711 telephone interviews with people aged 18 and over across Great Britain on Thursday night, Friday and Saturday.

SUNDAY TIMES

"There was clear evidence yesterday of concerted efforts by Mrs Thatcher and her ministers to pull together the threads of European policy which they now see as the crucial threat to Tory unity and recovery."

Major pledges to fight Delors plan but hints at ERM progress

Mr John Major, the Chancellor, yesterday pledged Britain's determination to fight all the way against the Delors Report proposals for European economic and monetary union. But he insisted that Britain was not foot-dragging on Europe and signalled his readiness for British membership of the exchange rate mechanism of the European Monetary system.

Although the new Chancellor set about the Delors proposals in a Commons debate as involving an unacceptable centralist European control of domestic economic policies, he also published a document fleshing out proposals for a gradualist, marketed coordination of economic policies outlined by his predecessor, Mr Nigel Lawson, as Britain's own contribution to the debate.

There was clear evidence yesterday of concerted efforts by Mrs Thatcher and her senior ministers to pull together the threads of the European policy which they now see as the crucial threat to Tory unity and recovery.

Ministers were keen to let it be known that the Cabinet, in the first sign of a newly-collective approach, had yesterday morning a brief debate and approved Mr Major's plan. Mrs Thatcher herself responded to a planted question with a carefully crafted form of words designed to satisfy both wings of the party. And Mr Major's speech in the debate was said afterwards to have united Conservative Europhobes and Europhiles by making clear Britain's willingness to cooperate with Europe while underlining that there could be no question of signing away national sovereignty on economic policy.

Mr Major told MPs that such control was fundamental to Britain's Parliamentary constitution and practice "and it is not a matter that can be bargained away or cast aside".

Putting forward his own plan, the new Chancellor rejected virtually every element in the Delors Report, accepted by the last European Council in Madrid as a basis for further action.

He said that Community rules on the use of national budget deficits were neither necessary nor desirable. He condemned the idea of a European system of central banks with sole responsibility for Community monetary and exchange rate policy as making no provision for the accountability to national parliaments or national governments, who would still be held responsible for such policies by their electorates.

Mr Major's own proposals started from the three principles of seeking price stability, increasing the influence of markets and competition, and retaining the maximum possible level of national control over economic policy-making.

He intends to present them to his European counterparts at a meeting on Monday week.

THE TIMES

John Major in action in the House of Commons

Interest rates could rise if necessary: Chancellor

A sliding pound in the financial markets did not help John Major in his efforts to restore calm.

MR MAJOR, the Chancellor, said yesterday he was "quite ready to raise interest rates if I consider it necessary". His comments, in an interview with The Daily Telegraph, followed a further sharp fall in the pound in London.

Sterling dropped nearly two pfennigs to DM2.77 against the German currency before recovering after Bank of England support. It closed virtually unchanged at DM2.7920, and gained nearly half a cent to $1.5680.

The early slide reflected City concerns that Mr Major was reluctant to raise rates to defend the pound for fear of precipitating recession.

Mr Major insisted that he did take the pound into account, and was prepared to raise base rates above 15 per cent if needed. But he did not believe he should look at the exchange rate "in a mechanistic way".

Sterling has fallen by nearly four per cent since he took office. His reluctance to raise base rates in response has been suspected by the City to indicate a change in policy.

However, Mr Major stressed that he "strongly supported Nigel Lawson's policies while I was at the Treasury as Chief Secretary". He added: "And I see no reason to change my view now."

The Chancellor was urged to resist pressure for higher interest rates, despite the fall in sterling, by the independent National Institute for Economic and Social Research.

The institute's latest review provides some support for the Chancellor, who has been criticised for his policy of "benign neglect" towards sterling.

City anxiety has centred on the inflationary dangers of the sharp fall in sterling, and on the possibility that higher import costs will

DAILY TELEGRAPH

"I strongly supported Nigel Lawson's policies while I was at the Treasury as Chief Secretary, and I see no reason to change my view now."

John Major

make the balance of payments position even worse in the short term. This could provoke a downward spiral in international confidence, some analysts say.

The institute concedes that Mr Major has taken office at a difficult time and outlook for the future describes the economy as "sombre". It says policy had gone far enough. "The time is now past, in our view, for tightening policy to reduce domestic demand.

"The growth in the economy has already slowed down and the pressure of demand is falling. If that tendency were now reinforced by yet higher interest rates the outcome could well be a recession rather than merely a pause in expansion."

Like the Chancellor, the institute expects the economy to slow rapidly next year, with domestic product increasing by 1.6 per cent and by under one if North Sea activity is excluded. A weaker pound should boost exports, according to the institute, but the current account gap will only narrow slightly, from £21 billion this year to £17.9 billion next. The Treasury is forecasting a contraction in the deficit to £15 billion in 1990. Progress on inflation will be hampered by the effect of a falling pound and the continuation of high wage settlements.

The increased emphasis which the Chancellor appears to place on fiscal policy is welcomed by the institute.

"We would certainly recommend that the excessive reliance on high interest rates be abandoned." Instead, the institute recommends that there should be a progressive shift in the policy mix over the next few years towards relatively tighter fiscal policy and a relatively less tight monetary policy.

However, interest rates are unlikely to come down very fast.

The institute foresees a cut of one per cent to 14 per cent towards the end of next year.

John Major works at home on Budget papers.

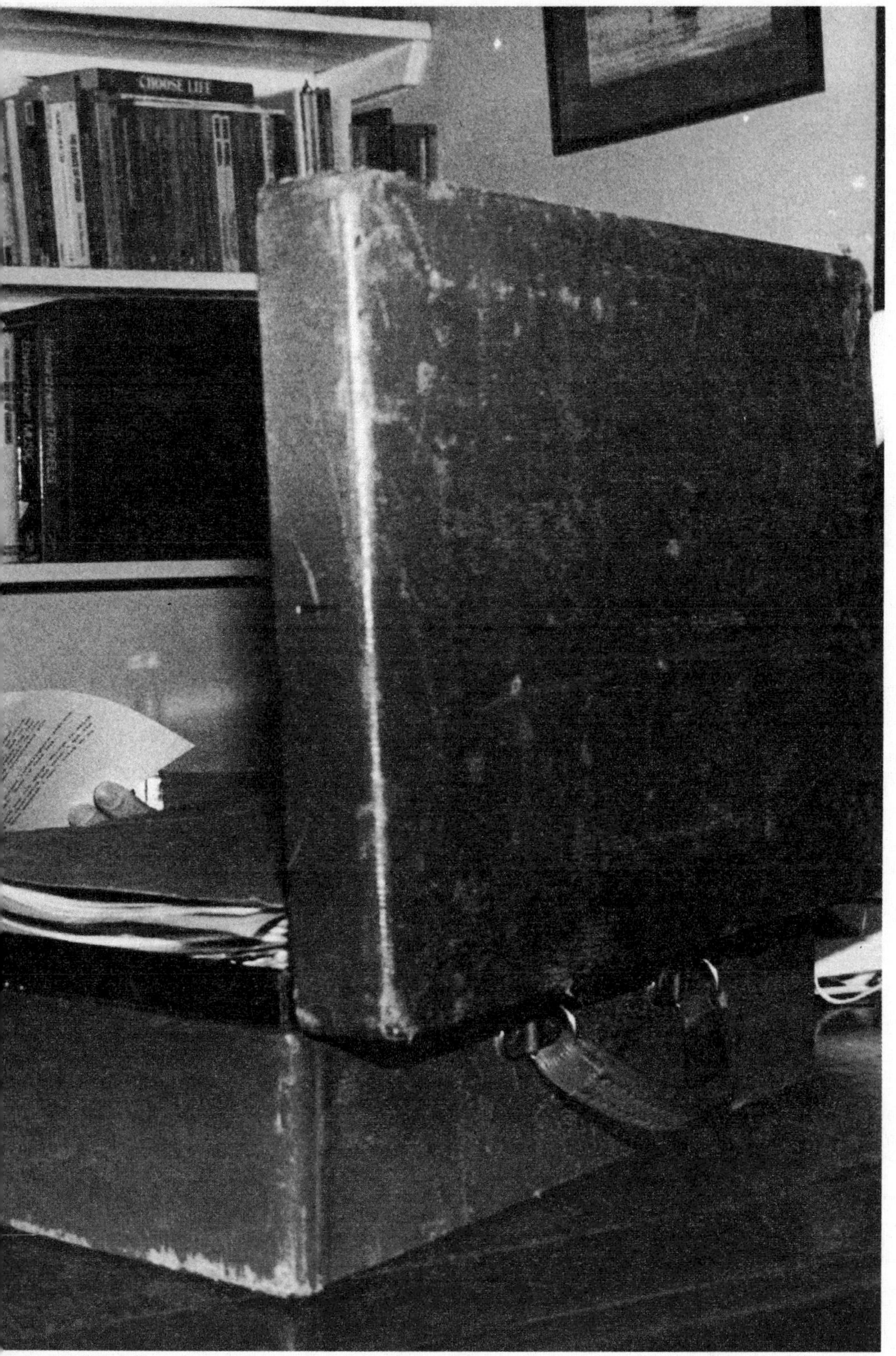
CHOOSE LIFE

It was a cleverly constructed and brilliantly presented Budget speech, according to The Times, and all the more significant for being seen live for the first time by millions watching on television. But other reactions from sections of industry, commerce and the unions called it a Budget of missed opportunities. It made John Major more friends – and those opposed to his ideas were never likely to be friends anyway.

THE BUDGET: Major tries to draw sting from poll tax and boost savings – extra on drink, smoking, petrol and company cars

By GEORGE JONES, Political Editor

MR MAJOR, the Chancellor, lifted the gloom among Tory MPs yesterday with a skilfully-packaged Budget which coupled the first overall increase in taxation since 1981 with radical measures to encourage saving and take the sting out of the introduction of the poll tax next month.

Delivering his first Budget, Mr Major did not disguise the bleak economic outlook this year – with inflation likely to go over nine per cent, interest rates staying high for some time to come, and the risk of a 'quite sharp' downturn in the economy – though he held out the prospect of significant improvements by the middle of 1991.

He described it as a 'Savers' Budget' which took no risk with inflation. He increased excise duties, with rises above the rate of inflation for petrol, spirits and cigarettes, but the squeeze was less severe than had been forecast, increasing the yield from taxation by £500 million next year and just under £1 billion in 1991.

The main income tax allowances will also be raised in line with the cost of living, disappointing some Tory MPs who had been hoping for a clearer signal that the Chancellor was ready to take tough action to bear down on inflation.

But those worried that Mr Major had not done enough to reassure the financial markets were heavily outnumbered by Tory backbenchers who felt the Chancellor had acted imaginatively – in a year when his options were severely limited – to meet criticisms of the Government's policies and to begin the long haul to restore the Conservatives' fortunes.

The biggest cheer, with Tory MPs waving their Order papers, came when Mr Major announced the doubling from £8,000 to £16,000 in upper limit of savings people can have before they lose entitlement for rebates on the poll tax and other social security benefits.

This has been a significant grievance in MPs' postbags and the Chancellor was later praised by several leading critics of the community charge for 'listening' to their complaints and signposting the way for further changes in the poll tax.

But the Chancellor's speech was interrupted for the third year running – this time by angry Scots MPs demanding that the poll tax concessions should be made retrospective in Scotland where the community charge has been in operation for a year.

MPs of all parties also welcomed the extra financial aid for football safety, the increased help for the blind, a Gift Aid Scheme for charities and the ending of taxation of workplace nurseries as small but important trimmings which would bring benefits much in excess of their cost to the Exchequer. The measures to boost savings were seen as a long – overdue reform to give more encouragement to thrift at a time when runaway credit is a major factor in the inflationary boom.

DAILY TELEGRAPH

The traditional pose as John Major leaves Number 11 Downing Street wwith his wife on his way to the House of Commons to present the 1990 Budget.

'We are back in business,' said one Tory MP last night. At a private meeting of the backbench Conservative finance committee, Mr Major was given an enthusiastic reception from MPs after telling them to keep their nerve.

'If we don't lose our heads, we won't lose our majority,' said Mr Major.

But there was a critical reception from Opposition MPs with Mr Kinnock, Labour leader – though forced to begin his response by welcoming several of the concessions announced by Mr Major – describing it as a 'bits and pieces' Budget which was too late to save the Government.

Dr Marjorie Mowlam, Labour's City spokesman, said Mr Major was holding on by his fingernails, hoping things would get better. 'The immediate reaction of the City on hearing the Budget was to start selling. This is the clearest indicator possible that the Budget was not what the City needed.' Mr Alan Beith, the Liberal Democrats' Treasury spokesman, said it was a Budget for 'endless mortgage misery' and the Chancellor had failed to face up to the tough decisions that were needed.

Dr David Owen, the SDP leader, accused Mr Major of taking considerable risks with inflation, which could lead to the whole Budget strategy coming unstuck.

The Chancellor had begun his 1hr 25min Budget speech, which was shorn of much of the usual Treasury jargon for the benefit of television viewers watching it for the first time, with a declaration of intent that he would take no risks with inflation and maintain a strong fiscal surplus.

But he also warned that things would get worse before they got better. The poll tax would add more than one per cent to the Retail Price Index next month, while the increases in excise duties would add at least another 0.5 per cent.

Although Mr Major did not say at what level inflation – currently running at 7.7 per cent – will peak, it is likely to go over nine per cent before falling back to a little over seven per cent by the end of this year.

He predicted it would drop below five per cent in 1991, though at a press conference last night, he admitted that progress in reducing inflation had been 'frustratingly slow'.

'A significant fall is still some months away and a number of factors will mean that the position will worsen noticeably before it improves,' said Mr Major.

He was equally bleak on interest rates, offering no early relief for home-owners facing record mortgage interest payments. They would stay high for some time to come as to reduce them prematurely, only to increase them again, would be extremely damaging.

Although optimistic about the longer-term prospects for British industry, Mr Major forecast that the economy would grow by only one per cent this year because of the squeeze on inflation. The downturn, he admitted, might become quite sharp, but he was confident the period of low growth would be short-lived – and it should rise again next year to around 2.75 per cent.

Although Mr Major's options were limited, he sought to make his mark in his first Budget by promising to abolish two taxes – stamp duty on share transactions and the composite rate tax which is levied on building society and bank interest payments.

For the first time for nine years there is an increase in taxation, and the Budget small print shows that the well-off, who were a principal beneficiary of Mr Lawson's largesse, will be hurt the most as the threshold at which they pay higher rate tax at 40 per cent will not be uprated in line with inflation.

Mr Lawson's policy of freezing excise duties – the tax on spirits has not been increased since 1985 – has also been abandoned because it was distorting the tax system. Mr Major has also bowed to pressure from Tory MPs and Ministers, firmly resisted by his predecessor, to exempt workplace nurseries from taxation to help more mothers return to work.

The changes in the tax structure designed to encourage savings are Mr Major's main Budget reform. After firing a warning shot at the banks and building societies for sending out too many 'mail shots' encouraging people to borrow, he outlined a range of incentives targeted at the mass of 'ordinary taxpaying savers' – ranging from children with pocket money to pensioners.

From next January, every adult will be entitled to one tax exempt special savings account, Tessa for short, on which their capital will be able to earn tax free interest over a period of five years.

The other side of John Major is an ardent fan of Britain's summer and winter games: cricket and Association Football. A supporter of Chelsea and a follower of Surrey since childhood, he ingeniously combined his role in politics with his support for Surrey's youth year.

No flannelling

Chancellors should be adept at raising cash but just who does John Major think will be prepared to stump up £10,000 for the pleasure of a seat at his dinner table? That is the "maximum sum" the Chancellor has suggested for a series of private fund raising dinners at his Downing Street residence in aid of Surrey County Cricket Club's youth year of which he is patron.

The club said yesterday that "the fee will be the subject of a some gentle negotiation", but with Major offering to host dinner for 14 at a time, each event could raise more than £100,000 towards the £500,000 target. Major is determined to be a working patron. When he took the post, he startled the organisers by announcing: "There is no point in having a donkey if it does not pull the cart."

The cricket-crazy Chancellor, a long-standing Surrey member, hosted a cocktail party this week for the appeal attended by such cricketing greats as Colin Cowdrey, Sir Leonard Hutton, Alec Bedser and Peter May. When, the assembled cricketers wanted to know, was he expecting promotion from number 11 to number 10?

THE TIMES

"I think he will be well able to do it and I think his style, his courteous and friendly style, will go down very well in the European Community."

Sir Leon Brittan

The "hard Ecu" was John Major's answer to calls for currency union. It was proposed as a pan-European unit operating alongside national currencies for use in business and by travellers.

Major claiming EC support for 'hard ecu' plan

By BORIS JOHNSON, EC Correspondent, in Brussels

MR MAJOR, the Chancellor, said last night that support was taking off in Europe for Britain's 'hard ecu' alternative to the Delors plan for a single European bank and currency. Britain is mounting an urgent campaign to prevent the EC from adopting the Delors plan.

Mrs Thatcher has said it would be 'the greatest transfer of sovereignty we have ever known'.

Signs are growing that the campaign is paying off. 'Our ideas are being taken as of very great interest indeed,' said Mr Major after a meeting of EC finance ministers agreed to debate the British proposal.

The Whitehall view appears to be gaining ground as a sudden burst of nervousness that they could be left behind in the second group of a divided Europe seizes the weaker economies of the community.

A Spanish diplomat said: 'If Delors means a two-speed Europe, we should try something else.' The fears of the poorer countries were fuelled yesterday by a report from the EC's monetary committee suggesting that monetary union could be staggered.

The chairman of the German Bundesbank, Herr Karl-Otto Pohl, recently proposed that Germany, France and the Benelux countries might be ready to advance rapidly to a single currency.

Mr Major disclosed yesterday that he will visit Spain, Portugal and other poorer countries, and he will urge them to understand that the high-speed Delors approach could break up the EC.

The British plan for a 'hard ecu' – a parallel currency which could be used by businessmen and travellers without abolishing national currencies such as sterling or the franc – is intended to soften the economic shock for the weaker countries.

The Chancellor said: 'If we moved rapidly to a single currency there would be strains and tensions, and four or five countries said they were genuinely concerned about the lack of economic convergence.' A single currency would prevent governments devaluing to combat unemployment.

The hard ecu will be discussed at a special meeting of the EC's monetary committee on September 4. But the meeting may be its last chance to win round the majority of the EC, which still sees the ultimate goal as a single currency.

The German Finance Minister, Herr Theo Waigel, said the proposal 'had interesting elements', but Germany and others want to go further.

DAILY TELEGRAPH

Ringing the Lutine Bell at Lloyds to mark Euro Day, 2nd July 1990.

No move this weekend on pound

There was constant speculation in the City that Britain was about to join the Exchange Rate Mechanism as recession drifted ever closer.

By ANNE SEGALL, Economics Correspondent

STERLING will not join the European exchange rate mechanism this weekend, the Chancellor of the Exchequer said yesterday as he prepared to fly to Rome for talks with European finance ministers.

Mr Major warned that inflation figures next week will show a rise above 10 per cent, which would be the highest for more than eight years, and that it would be unsafe to cut interest rates too soon.

The Chancellor was unwilling to encourage further market speculation by allowing himself to be drawn on a likely date for British membership. But he made clear it was just a matter of time. The decision to join had been taken and the Government was simply waiting for the inflation conditions set for entry to be met.

'I think there is no doubt in anyone's mind that we have crossed the Rubicon, that we have decided that we will join the ERM,' he

Karl-Otto Pohl, president of the Bundesbank, visits Number 11 Downing Street.

told the BBC's Today programme.

Dearer oil and the effect of the drought on the price of fresh food were threatening to push inflation above 10 per cent from the present 9.8 per cent, he said. This is more than twice the average for members of the exchange rate system.

Speculative fever has gripped the City in the run-up to the Rome meeting which is also being attended by European central bank governors.

Expectations had reached such a pitch that economists throughout the City were being asked to make themselves available over the weekend to handle inquiries.

According to Mr Major, there are now clear signs the economic squeeze has begun to work, but that did not spell recession and he felt it was too early to cut interest rates.

The purpose of policy is to get the rate of inflation not just down, but down very dramatically, continuing to head down and make sure that it stays down.' He would use his judgment to decide when the policy could be relaxed.

The Chancellor's warning that interest rates will remain at 15 per cent, a rate which has held for almost a year, followed a Bank of England decision on Thursday to reverse a decline in money

GUARDIAN

market rates associated with expectations of ERM membership. The Bank sent a clear signal that whatever the outcome of the meeting at the weekend, membership of the ERM should not be seen as an automatic trigger for lower borrowing costs.

Mr Major is believed to have effectively ruled out membership of the European currency block this month and is now expected to delay a decision until he delivers his Autumn Statement in November. He could even wait until the start of the inter-governmental conference on European economic union in December.

Mr Peter Spencer, chief UK economist at Shearson Lehman, welcomed Mr Major's decision given the uncertainties created by the Gulf crisis and the strains of unification in Germany. Sterling's petrocurrency status would make it difficult to hold sterling steady within the European system.

'It is my view that Mr Major should sit pat on 15 per cent base rates and remain outside the ERM until some of these uncertainties resolve themselves,' he said.

There is concern, too, that higher headline inflation will encourage a wages explosion this winter, with workers attempting to match the inflation-plus deals secured by the car unions. This would push earnings well into double figures, which would put industry under considerable competitive pressure.

On the exchanges, the pound had a bumpy ride, closing lower on the day as speculative positions were unwound. Dealers also reported large sales of sterling out of the Middle East, probably by Gulf states needing to raise dollars for defence purposes. At the close, the pound was showing a loss of 1.30 cents to $1.8940.

Mr Tim Fox, a Midland Bank currency strategist, said Mr Major's statement had helped to clear the air and would be seen as helpful by international investors. After a nervous start, share prices recovered, with the Financial Times 100 share index closing two points higher at 2122.9.

Opposite, *the Chancellor speaking at the Lord Mayor's Banquet at the Mansion House to the grandees of the City of London.*

Britain's eventual decision to join the European Exchange Rate Mechanism on the first day of the Tory Party conference came as a complete surprise to the markets, and the accompanying cut in interest rates was more than welcome to Britain's beleaguered home-owners and businesses.

Sterling's Entry into the ERM

Major plays ERM ace: shares soar as Government seizes political and economic initiative by applying for membership of the European Exchange Rate Mechanism and announcing a one-point cut in interest rates from Monday

By Anthony Bevins, Colin Brown, Peter Torday, Peter Rodgers and David Usborne

THE GOVERNMENT last night seized the political and economic initiative by applying for membership of the European Exchange Rate Mechanism and announcing a one-point cut in interest rates from Monday, the day before the Conservative conference begins.

The bold move – which stunned the financial markets and sent share values soaring – signals the Prime Minister's determination to break the Labour lead and her hopes that it will pave the way for a fourth election victory within the next 12 months.

The decision caught Labour politicians by surprise, and took the gloss off their conference week. It will put a shine into Conservative expectations for what could now well be the last conference before the next election.

The Treasury announcement came just after 4pm, within hours of the concluding rendition of the Red Flag and Jerusalem at the Labour conference in Blackpool; Roy Hattersley, the deputy Labour leader, commented: 'The coincidence is almost beyond belief.' Neil Kinnock, the Labour leader, said it was right to cut interest rates and join the ERM, but said it was the 'action of a cornered government'.

John Major, Chancellor of the Exchequer, last night responded by insisting that his judgment had been taken exclusively on economic rather than political grounds – the time was ripe. He went on to say: 'If we had chosen last weekend, which was a possibility, people would have said we were seeking to wreck the Labour Party conference. We couldn't have chosen next weekend for a whole variety of technical reasons. We were driven back into this weekend, or a considerable period of delay. I did not think delay was right. This weekend, therefore, was clearly signalled.' But by ruling out last weekend on the grounds that it clashed with Labour's conference, Mr Major was clearly conceding that political considerations played a part, and even if he did not have his eye on next week in Bournemouth, his Cabinet colleagues and the party faithful will delight in a decision which could mark a turning point in the party fortunes.

If that change occurs, and the Conservatives begin to overtake Labour in the opinion polls, Margaret Thatcher has made it quite clear that she will go to the country in the hope of winning a fourth term. If that cannot be achieved by next summer, which is doubted, it could be possible in 12 months' time, at which point Mrs Thatcher could call an election. Speaking outside No 10 Downing Street last night, Mrs Thatcher said the decisions to cut interest rates and join the ERM had been made possible because Conservative policies were working.

'They are seen to be working from CBI surveys, from the fall in retail sales, from the fall in the sale of cars and, above all, from monetary conditions. All this makes it quite clear that we are in a position to reduce interest rates from 15 per cent to 14 per cent.' The Prime Minister stressed the most important aim remained getting inflation down but said the move would 'underpin our anti-inflationary stance', adding that Britain's inflation rate, for so long the sticking-point in the Government's refusal to join the ERM, would drop nearer the European average 'in the coming months'.

Mrs Thatcher said she hoped the move would lead to reduced mortgage rates.

Asked if she had taken the decision to avoid a recession, she replied: 'We have the interest rate, which we put up just almost a year ago this weekend to 15 per cent, to tackle inflation. Tackling inflation is tough, it leads to tough times for some people, but you have to do it to take inflationary pressures out. There are clear signs that inflationary pressures are being reduced and therefore it is time to take the interest rate down.' The pound will enter the ERM at a central rate of 2.95 marks, the dominant currency in the system. However, Mr Major said last night that entry could be negotiated at an even higher rate. Unlike all other EC currencies, which – apart from the Spanish peseta – fluctuate within narrow margins, it will be allowed to trade within wide 6 per cent margins against the other eight ERM currencies.

The Government will enforce the fluctuation margins by stepping into the currency markets with other European central banks, buying the pound when it weakens and selling it when grows too strong. In times of violent currency swings, the Government could be driven into more frequent interest rate increases or reductions than the domestic economy alone might warrant.

The one-point reduction in interest rates to 14 per cent was seen as an urgent response to cries of alarm at recession from industry, the clearing banks and the City. Analysts said the cut indicated that the Treasury's forecasts for the economy, due to be published next month, were probably far worse than had been imagined.

Sir Leon Brittan, Britain's senior member of the European Commission, said: 'This is good news for Britain and good news for Europe. It will help the fight against inflation and is good for British business. It shows the clear commitment of the UK to a successful completion of stage one of economic and monetary union.' Jacques Delors, president of the European Commission, also welcomed the move and said it should help Britain reduce its rate of inflation. He added, however, that he would wait and see whether Britain's decision would signal a new commitment to the EC, and in particular to EMU.

Mrs Thatcher said last night that the decision did not signal any softening of government hostility to full European monetary union – 'not in any way at all. They know full well we are totally against the single currency, and so is our Parliament. Government and party are as one.' The former Chancellor Nigel Lawson said last night: 'I warmly welcome this historic decision, which I have long advocated. While ERM membership is no panacea, it provides the essential missing link in the Government's economic policy and will prove of increasing benefit to the British economy.'

INDEPENDENT

It took more than ten years of British membership of the European Monetary System before John Major took the plunge into the ERM.

CITY: Decade of waiting

1979: Britain joins newly-created European Monetary System but sterling kept out of exchange rate mechanism.

1979-1985: Treasury firmly opposed to entry.

1985: Nigel Lawson argues that it is time to enter. Prime Minister and her personal economic adviser Sir Alan Walters strongly opposed.

1986: Pound allowed to fall sharply, ending the year at Dm2.850

1987: World finance ministers agree to keep all the world's main currencies stable. Lawson begins to 'shadow' German mark – the key ERM currency.

1988: Pound rises above shadow ceiling of three marks, touching Dm3.225. Interest rates cut to 7.5 pc. Then shadowing abandoned as rates rise to 12 pc.

1989:
February – Pound rises to high of Dm3.2725.
April – Lawson rejects Delors committee report outlining steps towards economic and monetary union.
June – Lawson signals 1990 as possible date for full entry into EMS. Thatcher agrees Britain will enter when inflation is more in line with European rates.
September – Walters continues to criticise ERM. Split between Thatcher and Lawson deepens.
October – Lawson resigns as Chancellor. Walters follows suit. John Major becomes Chancellor. Interest rates at 15 pc, economy weakens. Businessmen urge ERM membership to stabilise pound.
December – Pound falls to low of Dm2.7225.

1990: Pressure builds to join ERM.
May – Prime Minister drops her veto on full entry into EMS.
June – Major proposes new European currency for use by businessmen and tourists as a radical alternative plan for monetary union.
July – Walters publishes book condemning ERM.
September – Major reaffirms his commitment to Britain joining ERM 'at earliest possible date'.
October – Pound at Dm2.9300. ERM entry announced. Base rate cut by 1 pc to 14 pc.

DAILY TELEGRAPH

Practising woodwork on a visit to a constituency school.

6

Party Leader

For nine November days, Margaret Thatcher watched helplessly as the tide of politics turned irresistibly against her.

Loyalty from her closest allies was to no avail as, first from Number 10, then from the Paris summit, she watched Michael Heseltine's campaign get under way. When the result of the first leadership ballot emerged, despite her first reaction to "fight and fight to win", it was clear that the discontent among her fellow Tory MPs made it impossible for her to remain as Prime Minister.

There were tears as one by one she consulted her Cabinet ministers, there were tears the following morning when she told them she had decided to resign, and her face crumpled again as she left Downing Street to tell the Queen that she was intending to resign.

But the principal perpetrator of the fatal wound, Heseltine, was not to triumph. Instead, the John Major bandwagon rolled towards victory.

Punchbag hits back and leaves PM reeling

By Philip Stephens, Political Editor

AT 11am yesterday, Mrs Margaret Thatcher berated Sir Geoffrey Howe in front of his cabinet colleagues. Eight hours later the man who had begun to look like her punchbag had hit back – and left the prime minister reeling.

During the weekly cabinet meeting, senior ministers had watched incredulously another of the embarrassing exchanges between the prime minister and her deputy which for months had left them barely on speaking terms.

Ironically this time it had nothing to do with Europe – the issue on which Sir Geoffrey resigned. In spite of Britain's isolation at the Rome summit at the weekend and Mrs Thatcher's tempestuous performance in the Commons on Tuesday, that issue was not even on the cabinet's agenda.

Mrs Thatcher instead attacked Sir Geoffrey over his organisation of the legislative programme for the Queen's Speech on Wednesday. As leader of the Commons it was his job to prepare that programme.

Her complaint was apparently so trivial that others could not understand what the fuss was about. But it may well have been the final ignominy for a politician who had served the premier for 15 years but bitterly opposed her on what he regards as the most important issue facing Britain in the 1990s – its place in Europe.

After talking with a few close friends yesterday, Sir Geoffrey went to 10 Downing Street and resigned. He told Mrs Thatcher he could no longer support her hostile opposition to European integration. He wanted the freedom to express his views from the backbenches.

There was no question of any bargaining. He had decided to go and was not there to strike any deal on the terms on which he might stay.

FINANCIAL TIMES

Years at the Foreign Office preceded by a long spell as Chancellor had convinced Sir Geoffrey Howe of the need for closer ties with Europe. Mrs Thatcher saw those strengthening ties as a threat to sovereignty and was convinced of the need for a comparatively arms-length relationship on some Community issues, particularly on the development of the Exchange Rate Mechanism. Bound by collective Cabinet responsibility, Sir Geoffrey took a typically careful look at his options – then resigned.

5

Sir Geoffrey has pondered his future in the government since July last year when it was Mrs Thatcher who summoned him to Downing Street during her cabinet reshuffle. She told him that he must move from the foreign office.

She offered him first the choice of becoming home secretary or, the job he took, leader of the House of Commons.

He won also the additional title of deputy prime minister but hours later Mrs Thatcher's aides were making clear that it gave him no extra authority.

Within months, the message from Downing Street was that the prime minister could not stand to be in the same room as her deputy. When they sat side by side in the Commons they rarely exchanged a word.

Behind their estrangement lay Europe. It was Sir Geoffrey's alliance with Mr Nigel Lawson, the former chancellor, to force Mrs Thatcher into accepting the so-called 'Madrid conditions' for Britain's entry into the EMS exchange rate mechanism, that led to his demotion.

Three months later – and just over a year ago – Mr Lawson dramatically quit as chancellor. Sir Geoffrey stayed on.

The success of Mr John Major, the chancellor, in persuading Mrs Thatcher last month finally to take sterling into the ERM had cheered him up. Perhaps there was hope of compromise on Europe.

That hope evaporated in Rome at the weekend and in the Commons on Tuesday. Mrs Thatcher alone among the 12 refused to sign up for a timetable for European monetary and economic union.

Then at Westminster she launched a passionate onslaught against the alleged determination of the European Commission and Britain's European partners to strip her government of its currency and its sovereignty. The implication was that, if necessary, Mrs Thatcher was prepared to fight the election draped in the Union Flag.

Sir Geoffrey had had enough. His chances of succeeding the prime minister, who he had served as her first chancellor, had anyway evaporated. He saw no prospect of persuading her from the inside of the need to make the accommodations with Europe that Mr Hurd and Mr Major are also pressing. So he quit.

His friends last night made clear there was no question of Sir Geoffrey challenging Mrs Thatcher for the leadership later this month. They left the impression however that he would not shed any tears if his departure paved the way for someone else to do just that.

Sir Geoffrey and Lady Howe.

It was all the more lethal for the careful, measured tones of delivery. It was all the more damaging given the reputation of the speaker as a man of peace, a man of compromise and a man of patience. It confirmed the onset of the leadership battle and thus the beginning of the end of the Thatcher years.

Ex-minister savages Thatcher's 'nightmare images' of Europe
Heseltine to throw hat in ring today • Kinnock demands poll

Howe assault puts PM on battle alert

By MICHAEL WHITE, Political Editor

MARGARET Thatcher and her embattled supporters were last night clearing the decks for mortal battle after Sir Geoffrey Howe had offered a stunned House of Commons the most damning indictment of a prime minister by a senior colleague in living memory. Many Tories now believe she cannot recover from it – even if the party can.

As astonished MPs struggled to absorb the sheer vehemence of Sir Geoffrey's 18-minute statement it was all but universally expected that Michael Heseltine would today announce his long-expected bid for the Tory leadership, claiming that the crisis exposed with brutal candour by the Howe speech justified his abandonment of pledges not to challenge Mrs Thatcher directly.

The Labour leader, Neil Kinnock, said last night that Sir Geoffrey had shown the Tories to be divided and unfit to govern. He called for an immediate general election. 'It is the sovereign right of the people of this country to determine who governs Britain, not the special privilege of Conservative MPs.' Mr Heseltine's allies, delighted by the blow at the Prime Minister's waning authority, were prudently cautious about the extent of his bandwagon. Few will predict whether they can achieve the necessary 157 votes to deprive Mrs Thatcher of outright victory in Tuesday's first ballot.

Mrs Thatcher let it be known she was 'saddened' by Sir Geoffrey's attack and, as in 1989, she appointed the former Defence Secretary, George Younger, to run her election campaign, despite his reported hesitation last week. He immediately led loyalists – many of them bitter against Sir Geoffrey for swamping the boat – in calls for no contest 'at this very critical time'. Heseltine supporters saw the appointment as a sign of panic.

Dissidents were preparing for a new leader, though it could be Douglas Hurd, not Mr Heseltine. Mr Hurd would only enter the frame if Mrs Thatcher was beaten or retired. As the unity candidate he would face not so much a second round as a rematch against Mr Heseltine.

The Prime Minister needs 50 per cent of the 372 eligible MPs' votes plus a 15 per cent – 56 votes – lead over any rival.

As loyalists did their sums some Heseltine enemies voiced two fears: that he would get at least 80 votes with up to 80 abstentions, not enough to stop Mrs Thatcher, but a deeply wounding defection by almost half the voting MPs; or that the Prime Minister's determination to fight to the last would

GUARDIAN

'The time has come for others to consider their response to the tragic conflict of loyalty with which I have myself wrestled for perhaps too long.'

'It is rather like sending your opening batsmen to the crease only for them to find ... that their bats have been broken before the game by the team captain.'

Sir Geoffrey Howe in the Commons yesterday

eventually deliver the crown to the challenger, not to Mr Hurd.

Even before Sir Geoffrey's speech, rightwingers detected a sea change in their colleagues' attitudes. Afterwards phrases like 'a public execution' and 'an Exocet' were used.

Sir Geoffrey had mixed generous praise with despair about a leader who sometimes saw Europe in terms of 'nightmare images' and as 'positively teeming with ill-intentioned people, scheming in her words "to extinguish democracy, to dissolve our national identities, to lead us through the back door into a federal Europe"'.

There were gasps and Labour laughter when he picked up Mrs Thatcher's defiant cricketing metaphor at Guildhall on Monday and lobbed it back.

Sending the Chancellor, John Major, in to argue for the Treasury's hard ecu formula after her sabotage was 'rather like sending your opening batsmen to the crease only for them to find the moment the first balls are bowled that their bats have been broken before the game by the team captain'.

As Mr Younger quickly pointed out, the former Deputy Prime Minister avoided endorsing Mr Heseltine. But, in the judgment of most MPs, he effectively invited his party to overthrow Mrs Thatcher when he concluded his speech by saying that the 'tragic conflict of loyalty' had become so great that he could no longer stay in the Cabinet.

'That is why I have resigned. In doing so I have done what I believe to be right for my party and my country,' he told the House. 'The time has come for others to consider their own response to the tragic conflict of loyalties with which I have myself wrestled for so long.' So bitterly personal was Sir Geoffrey's verdict on Mrs Thatcher, his ally of 20 years including 700 official meetings and 30 summits together, that it all but wiped out immediate comment on his crucial revelation about backstairs intrigue over the European policy dilemma, the heart of the crisis.

The revelation was, as long suspected, that he and the former Chancellor, Nigel Lawson – at his side yesterday – had threatened to resign if Mrs Thatcher had refused to accept the so-called Madrid Conditions of June 1989 for British entry into the European exchange rate mechanism (ERM).

Sir Geoffrey's thrust was that the pair knew that ERM membership, finally achieved by John Major last month, was essential to the control of inflation 'at least five years ago' and that the delay – the fault of Mrs Thatcher – had damaged both the Government and the economy.

The same dangers were now apparent over the moves towards Economic and Monetary Union, a subject on which Mr Heseltine had signalled a move back towards a more mainstream Tory position in the speech he made in Hamburg yesterday, before returning to hear Sir Geoffrey.

While expressing appropriate caution about the Delors plan for EMU, Sir Geoffrey also addressed the question of pooled sovereignty in Europe.

Again there was no comfort for Mrs Thatcher. 'We must at all costs avoid presenting ourselves yet again with an over-simplified choice, a false antithesis, a bogus dilemma between one alternative, starkly labelled 'co-operation between independent sovereign states', and a second, equally crudely labelled alternative, 'centralised federal super-state', as if there was no middle way.' Supporters of the Prime Minister, including the former party chairman, Norman Tebbit, were quick to express puzzlement about Sir Geoffrey's real differences of 'substance not tone' or to accuse him of wanting to fudge on Europe.

On ITV last night Kenneth Baker insisted that Mrs Thatcher remained 'the greatest asset of our country and our party' who would prevail.

30

The end came suddenly – a stark announcement from Number 10 that galvanised the whole country. Within minutes Douglas Hurd and John Major had declared their candidacies for the leadership and the stage was set for the campaign that would decide who was to be Britain's new Prime Minister.

Bravura end for Thatcher era: Resignation of Margaret Thatcher

By ROBIN OAKLEY AND PHILIP WEBSTER

A POLITICAL ERA ended yesterday when Margaret Thatcher announced that she would resign next week as prime minister. The foreign secretary, Douglas Hurd, and the Chancellor, John Major, immediately entered the Conservative leadership battle.

The prime minister, tears in her eyes, told the cabinet at 9am: 'I have concluded that the unity of the party and the prospects of victory at a general election would be better served if I stood down to enable cabinet colleagues to enter the ballot.'

She had decided overnight that she did not have the troops to win and urged cabinet colleagues to unite in electing one of their number to replace her, underlining her determination to stop Michael Heseltine.

Mrs Thatcher's departure brought her party an immediate opinion poll bonus. First results of a snap On-Line telephone poll of 760 voters for The Times last night showed that if Mr Heseltine were at the helm, 47 per cent would support the Tories, compared with 42 per cent for Labour. Under Mr Major, the figures were 45-44 and under Mr Hurd, the Tories would trail 44-45.

Of the three bandwagons, the one that appeared to be gathering speed fastest last night was that of Mr Major. His team went swiftly into action and his supporters were quickly joined by Norman Tebbit, who said: 'I am convinced that both left and right should unite under the leadership of John Major.' He hoped the 80 to 90 MPs who had promised to support him had he stood would now opt for Mr Major.

Mr Heseltine was one of the first to acknowledge the prime minister's 'awesome achievements'. He said: 'The important thing today is to pay tribute to the premiership of Margaret Thatcher. It has by any standards been remarkable. Perhaps the very fact that I at one moment found it impossible to continue in cabinet makes it particularly fitting for me to record the admiration and gratitude of the Conservative party for what she has achieved, and what so many of us worked so hard to help her bring about.'

President Bush telephoned Mrs Thatcher from Saudi Arabia last night, thanked her for all that she had done and signed off with the words: 'We love you.'

In the Commons and outside, MPs paid tribute to her as 'the greatest peacetime prime minister this century'. Even Neil Kinnock told her during question time that she amounted to more than those who had turned upon her.

Hoping for the best, Michael Heseltine and his wife before the leadership election.

The prime minister then put up a bravura performance in the censure debate, which ended with a 367-247 government victory. She was crisp, combative and humorous, winning universal cheers from Tories who could hardly believe that her reign had ended so messily.

There were recriminations from hard-core supporters who felt

THE TIMES

Mrs Thatcher and her husband, Denis, leave 10 Downing Street for the last time.

she had been betrayed by senior party figures.

Her decision to go has thrown the contest wide open. Mr Heseltine was continuing to win support yesterday, including that of the party deputy chairman, David Trippier. But some who voted for him in the first round did so only to ensure a second round involving Mr Hurd or Mr Major. Mr Heseltine now faces a battle to increase his first-round vote of 152 to the 187 required.

Some MPs would have preferred to see Mr Hurd and Mr Major agree which should be the 'cabinet unity' candidate to face Mr Heseltine. But instead they issued a joint statement saying: 'We have worked closely together in the recent past and will do so in the future. We have decided to let both our names go forward in friendly contest so that our party colleagues who take the decision can choose which of us is better placed to unite the party.'

Mr Major was seen as having an appeal that extended from the party mainstream to embrace the Thatcherite right, while Mr Hurd would have to compete with Mr Heseltine for the centre-left.

Mr Hurd said that he could 'heal the wounds before they go poisonous'. He denied that he and Mr Major were working to stop Mr Heseltine. 'We decided it was sensible to let Conservative MPs decide which of us were better able to unite the party. Divisions of the kind we have have had are disastrous.'

Mr Major said: 'I am in the business of the Conservative party winning the next election.' He regretted that the election was taking place, declaring: 'Mrs Thatcher has been a remarkable prime minister, a courageous advocate for change and a great world leader. I have been proud to support her. I believe history will judge her a great prime minister. I want to see the Conservative party remain in government and build on her achievements.'

Both indicated that they would address the problems of the poll tax, which Mr Heseltine has already made a key issue of his campaign.

Mr Heseltine has also made much of opinion polls showing that he was the best man to win the party the next election. The On-Line poll last night indicated that 36 per cent thought Mr Heseltine had the best chance of leading the Conservatives to victory; 27 per cent named Mr Hurd and 17 per cent Mr Major.

Mrs Thatcher's storming Commons performance had Conservative MPs, including some who had voted against her last Tuesday, standing and waving their order papers. In the lobbies afterwards several were tearful as they regretted her departure.

Mrs Thatcher laid into the Labour party with abandon, attacking Mr Kinnock's rhetoric. She spoke of her government's achievements 'rescuing Britain from the parlous state to which socialism has brought it'. She went on: 'Once again Britain stands tall in the counsels of Europe and of the world: and our policies have brought unparalleled prosperity to our citizens at home.' She predicted: 'We shall win a fourth general election. We shall win handsomely.'

As she warmed to her theme, she declared to laughter from all sides: 'I'm enjoying this.' She repeated her opposition to a European central bank and a single currency which was 'about the politics of Europe. It's about a federal Europe by the back door'.

Labour was not prepared to defend the rights of the British government. 'For them it's all compromise, sweep it under the carpet, leave it for another day, in the hope that the British people won't notice what's happening to them and how the powers will be gradually slipping away.'

Finally, Mrs Thatcher turned to the Gulf and said the time was fast approaching when the world would have to take more decisive action to compel President Saddam Hussein to leave Kuwait.

She recalled the Falklands conflict when she had dispatched forces to defend a small country. 'To those who have never had to take such decisions, may I say to them they are taken with a heavy heart, in the knowledge of the manifold dangers, but with tremendous pride in the professionalism and courage of our armed forces. But there is something else one feels as well. That is a sense of this country's destiny, the centuries of history and experience which ensure that when principles have to be defended, when good has to be upheld, when evil has to be overcome, then Britain will take up arms.'

Mr Tebbit said last night: 'After her performance this afternoon, the party feels very guilty, very sick and very ashamed of itself for what it has done.'

The Douglas Hurd campaign team before the second ballot in the leadership election.

John and Norma Major with their daughter, Elizabeth.

JOHN CAN WIN KEY TO No 10

Exclusive interview by Julian Makey

NORMA MAJOR spoke today of her excitement and anxiety as her Chancellor husband battles for Britain's top political job.

Mrs Major said her husband's campaign to become Prime Minister was like a cross between waiting for Christmas and an unpleasant trip to the dentist.

In an exclusive interview with the "News" at her Stukeley home, Mrs Major, 48, said she was confident that her husband could win.

But, just as she has done before in 18 months of political upheaval, she vowed to try to continue family life as normal.

"I am sure it is very naive of me but having been through the last 18 months which has been a difficult struggle, I would like to think we can carry on as we are. But whether the prospect is very realistic I do not know," she said.

She said that she felt her husband stood a good chance of becoming leader: "You do not go into these things without being positive about them."

She dismissed suggestions that her husband was too young and inexperienced for the job by saying he was roughly the same age as Labour leader Neil Kinnock, but by

"The campaign is like a cross between waiting for Christmas and an unpleasant trip to the dentist."

Norma Major

CAMBRIDGE EVENING NEWS

comparison had experience of top Government jobs.

In little more than a year, family life has been turned upside down.

First came Mr Major's appointment as Foreign Secretary. Then he was put in charge of running the economy.

Mrs Major, a lifelong Conservative, said she was upset by Mrs Thatcher's resignation.

"I am mortified. I think it is so sad. I am one of her biggest fans."

Mrs Major has always been keen to keep her family's political and private lives separate and wants to keep her daughter Elizabeth, 19, a trainee veterinary nurse, and son James, 15, who is still at school, out of the limelight.

"If the children were not still at home – and I am in no hurry to see them go – one may perhaps look at things in a different way," she said.

She hopes that if her husband does become Prime Minister, she will be able to use their home as a base and commute to Number 10 Downing Street and the premier's official country residence, Chequers, as required.

Mrs Major wants to continue her local WRVS Meals on Wheels round, and stay on as president of the local branch of Mencap, for which she has just raised £2,000 in a sponsored walk.

She is currently selling Christmas cards, gifts and wrapping paper to raise more money for the charity.

She said the campaign for the leadership of the party was exciting and she was being swept along by it.

She met her husband during the GLC election campaign in 1970 and they were married after a whirlwind summer romance.

But even she has been amazed by his rapid rise to the top.

Humble

"He dreamed of being Chancellor." she said. "We all fantasise don't we?"

Mr Major is billed in the leadership stakes as the man from a humble background whose father was a vaudeville trapeze artist.

But Mrs Major's own background was far from easy.

In a poignant moment, she revealed how she was named after her Army officer father, Norman, who was killed in a road accident in Belgium just a week after the end of the Second World War.

Her mother was left to bring her up on just £3 a week.

Politics even at the dining table.

As the Tory leadership election ended, a dramatic sequence of PA newsflashes began, spanning 15 minutes and culminating at 18.36 with the announcement that John Major was to be the new Prime Minister because there was not to be a third ballot between the three candidates.

PA reporters on station outside Mr Heseltine's home, in the Palace of Westminster and at the Foreign Office filed newsflashes on the withdrawal of the two losers in the second ballot, and on the announcement by the chairman of the 1922 Committee, Cranley Onslow, of John Major's succession to the office of Prime Minister.

```
Leadership Election:
PA LONDON

Transmitted on 27nov90 at 18:21
PA RUSH
PRI 2 PG 1 POLITICS Tory ()

PA NEWSFLASH: Major tops Tory
leader ballot but no outright
winner.
end mw

*

Transmitted on 27nov90 at 18:22
PA RUSH
PRI 2 PG 1 POLITICS Tory ()

PA NEWSFLASH: Voting: Major 185;
Heseltine 131; Hurd 56.

*
Transmitted on 27nov90 at 18:23
PA RUSH
PRI 2 PG 1 POLITICS Tory ()

PA NEWSFLASH: Third and final
ballot on Thursday.
end mw

*

Transmitted on 27nov90 at 18:24
PA RUSH
PRI 2 PG 1 POLITICS Tory ()

PA NEWSFLASH: Voting: Major 185;
Heseltine 131; Hurd 56.
end mw

*
Transmitted on 27nov90 at 18:25
PA RUSH
PRI 2 PG 1 POLITICS Tory ()

PA NEWSFLASH: Mr Heseltine says he
will vote for John Major in third
ballot.
end mw

*

Transmitted on 27nov90 at 18:28
PA RUSH
PRI 2 PG 1 POLITICS Tory ()

PA NEWSFLASH: Douglas Hurd also
declares that he will vote for John
Major in third ballot.
end mw
```

*

Transmitted on 27nov90 at 18:30
PA RUSH
PRI 2 PG 1 POLITICS Tory ()

PA NEWSFLASH: Mr Hurd says that "under the rather curious rules" there must be a third ballot, but he believes John Major is the right leader and he will vote for him.
end mw

*

Transmitted on 27nov90 at 18:32
PA RUSH
PRI 2 PG 1 POLITICS Tory ()

PA NEWSFLASH: HOW THEY VOTED
John Major: 185 (49.7% of 372 Tory MPs)
Michael Heseltine: 131 (35.2)
Douglas Hurd: 56 (15.1)

*

Transmitted on 27nov90 at 18:34
PA RUSH
PRI 2 PG 1 POLITICS Tory ()

PA NEWSFLASH: No third ballot, says Cranley Onslow, 1922 committee chairman.
end mw

*

Transmitted on 27nov90 at 18:36
PA RUSH
PRI 2 PG 1 POLITICS Tory ()

PA NEWSFLASH: Mr Major will therefore be the new Prime Minister.
end mw

*

Transmitted on 27nov90 at 18:41
PA RUSH
PRI 2 PG 1 POLITICS Tory ()

PA NEWSFLASH: Mrs Thatcher said to be "thrilled". She goes to No 11 and embraces Mr Major and congratulates him "most warmly".
end mw

*

A victory toast for John Major.

The defeated challenger, Michael Heseltine, leaving Number 1

after discussing his new job in John Major's Cabinet.

Mrs Thatcher's leadership ended officially the next morning when she tendered her resignation to the Queen. Shortly afterwards Mr Major visited Buckingham Palace to formalise his acceptance of office.

Heseltine and Hurd concede victory after Chancellor falls just short of majority

MAJOR WINS BATTLE FOR NO 10

New prime minister will be youngest since 1894

By Robin Oakley, Political Editor

JOHN Major, the 47-year-old Chancellor of the Exchequer who promised to create a truly classless society in the 1990s, is the new leader of the Conservative party. Today he will succeed Margaret Thatcher as prime minister, the youngest since Lord Rosebery in 1894.

Mrs Thatcher will see the Queen this morning to hand in her resignation. Forty-five minutes later, at 10.30, Mr Major will arrive at Buckingham Palace and be invited to form a government.

Michael Heseltine and Douglas Hurd, his rivals, conceded victory last night after Mr Major had come within two votes of the 187 required for outright victory. They called on the party to unite behind him and said they would vote for him in the third ballot. That ballot thus became a formality and was scrapped.

On the steps of 11 Downing Street, Mr Major said: 'This election has enhanced the democratic process substantially. It has been a very clean election and an election based on substance, not on personalities. It has dealt constructively with the issues.'

He expressed gratitude to his opponents for the way they had conducted the election and the gracious way they had conceded. 'It is a very exciting thing to become leader of the Conservative party, particularly exciting to follow one of the most remarkable leaders the Conservative party has had. I believe that as time proceeds and Margaret Thatcher's period as prime minister is seen in proper perspective it will be seen that she has been a very great prime minister, ' he said.

Mr Major added: 'My job is clear. We are going to unite. We are going to unite totally and absolutely and we will win the next general election.'

The voting in the second round of the contest was John Major 185, Michael Heseltine 131, Douglas Hurd 56. That gave Mr Major 49.7 per cent of the vote. Mr Major told Radio Cambridgeshire: 'We had an idea where our vote was coming from and we were not terribly surprised. I think I was pretty calm about it. There was great excitement and delight when it actually happened.'

Mr Heseltine, outside his Belgravia home, said his purpose was to ensure that unity was achieved at once 'in order that we may go on to win the next general election which will secure us a fourth term. We are about to see the dawn of a new era of Conservative administration.'

Douglas Hurd said Mr Major would be an excellent prime minister. 'I'm glad I had a go, I would have kicked myself if I

THE TIMES

hadn't had a go,' he said. 'But I've certainly come home a happy man tonight.'

Mrs Thatcher, who was seen peering out from the curtains of the Chancellor's home in Downing Street after the result was declared, said that she was 'thrilled'. She said that the Chancellor 'will be a superb leader of this country. I want everyone in the party to rally behind him so that he can go on and win a fourth successive general election.'

Mr Hurd and Mr Heseltine will meet Mr Major this morning. Last night, Mr Major was briefed by officials about the handover of power, and had a drink with Mrs Thatcher. At 10.15pm, he made his first appearance in the Commons as party leader. Conservative MPs cheered and waved their order papers and Neil Kinnock, the Labour leader, crossed the floor of the House to shake his hand.

Mr Kinnock, however, had greeted Mr Major's victory by saying: 'John Major is a Thatcherette. It means that the policies that brought poll tax, recession, heavy mortgages and rising unemployment will go on.'

Tory MPs greeted the swift end to the contest with jubilation. They said that Mr Heseltine's concession had done much to heal divisions and that the contest had united the party and transformed the prospects for the next election. Senior strategists do not expect Mr Major to go to the country until there has been a turn-around in the economy.

Mr Major confirmed beliefs that he would offer Mr Heseltine a job when he chatted to Tory MPs in the Commons. He was understood to have expressed gratitude over the way in which the campaigns were run, and added: 'I am going to have a cabinet of all their talents.'

MPs had been speculating that Mr Heseltine would be offered the post of Environment Secretary or Trade Secretary. Mr Hurd is

Conceding with grace, Michael Heseltine and his wife outside their Westminster home.

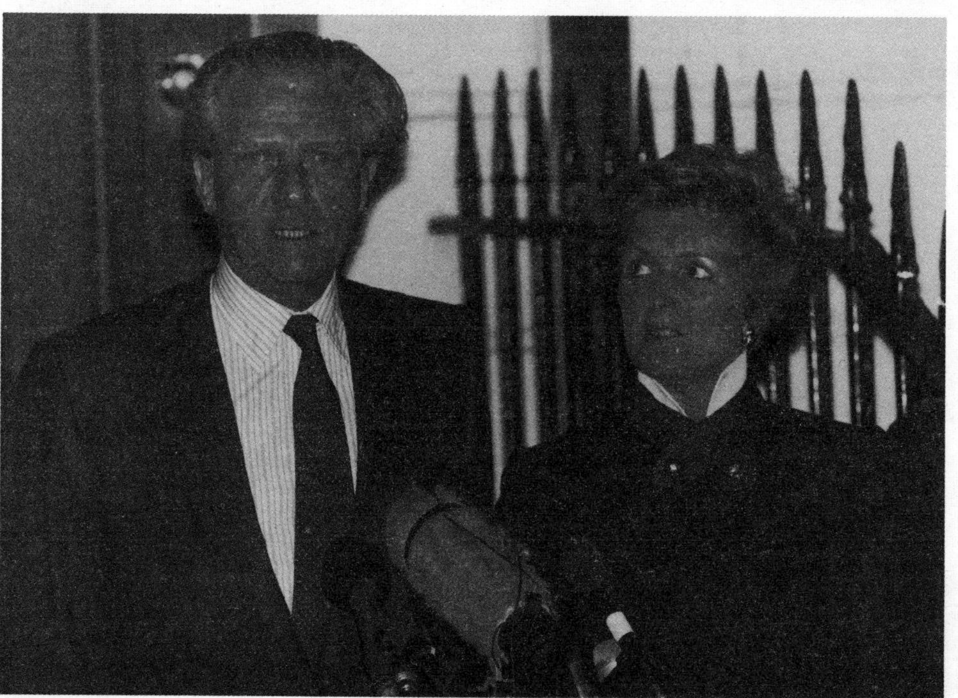

expected to be invited to continue as Foreign Secretary. Significantly, Lord Whitelaw, who had criticised Mr Heseltine, yesterday urged his inclusion in the cabinet.

Mr Major who has been only 11 years in the Commons and just three in the cabinet, has climbed swiftly. MPs acknowledge that few have risen so far and made so few enemies in the process.

He has emphasised his eagerness to boost education, and has said that he is prepared to see some increase in public expenditure to improve public services, but is committed to reducing the standard rate of income tax to 20p. The new prime minister will come under immediate pressure, however, for a poll tax review.

Sterling firmed slightly on foreign currency markets at the end of the leadership battle. Markets have been strengthening this week in the belief that base rates will be cut within a few days.

"I think that we can agree that any of the candidates, if they had been elected Prime Minister, would have been a different person by November next year."

Jim Cooper, chairman, Chester Conservative Association

A victory salute from John Major with his wife, Norma, at his side.

10

Huntingdon joy amid air of disaffection

By DAVID YOUNG

WHILE some of John Major's constituents in Huntingdon were aggravating their post-celebratory hangovers yesterday by blasting at pheasants on the Fens, others were suggesting that there was nothing to celebrate.

The constituency of Huntingdon is spread in a huge circle around the little market town and is predominantly wealthy, but there are pockets of urban decay, and local complaints about the poll tax are frequent enough for the local Conservative association offices to display a poster offering advice on how to claim rebates.

There are also many pensioners in the area who, as they eked out their housekeeping by making sure they picked the best of the crop at yesterday's market, said that they held out little prospect of their MP making any changes that would benefit them now that he is prime minister.

One said: 'He's a very good listener, but he hasn't actually done anything for the pensioner while he has been chancellor.' James Lomax, a painting and decorating instructor at Little Hay prison, near Huntingdon, and leader of the Labour group on Huntingdon district council, said: 'The constituency is right to take a certain pride in having its MP become prime minister, but he must also be made aware of the problems that exist in the area.

THE TIMES

A special handshake between John Major and his predecessor, Margaret Thatcher.

'There's considerable unemployment in some areas and the new prime minister won't be able to take any pride in the fact that in Huntingdon there are 19 homeless people now living in bed and breakfast accommodation provided by the social services, and that it is almost impossible to get in to the local hospital because of the long waiting list. The fact that Labour won two seats in the town in the last local elections must also tell him that everything is not rosy.' However, there are others who take the view that Mr Major has been an excellent constituency MP and will remain so. William Smith, a shop steward at a local engineering company and a shareholder in the firm because of Mrs Thatcher's policies, said: 'He really is a good local MP. He's in the area every weekend, and listens to everyone's problems.

'He has broad local appeal. He's a south Londoner and there's a large number of former south Londoners like me living in the Oxmoor Estate, which was built for the London overspill. He really is one of us.' However, just how accessible Mr Major will continue to be to local people remains to be seen. Already his home in the village of Stukeley nearby has a police guard, and 100 yards on either side of its entrance is now coned off.

Cambridgeshire police have said that they are drawing up contingency plans to deal with Mr Major's appearances in his constituency. The plans will probably be put to the test this weekend when Mr Major is expected briefly to return home, and then later in the week when he is due to attend the 21st anniversary dinner of the local Conservative club, the 80 tickets for which are now changing hands in a thriving black market.

As well as ensuring that the dinner will be a success, Mr Major is also assured of at least one more vote to add to his 27,000-odd majority. Roger Harding, the 52-year-old ticket collector at Huntingdon Station, said yesterday: 'I voted Labour all my life, but now John Major has been made prime minister he can have my vote at the next election.'

It was the scoop of a lifetime for Cambridge Evening News *reporter Julian Makey when he was invited into Number 11 with* News *photographer Roger Adams to conduct the first interview with the new Prime Minister designate.*

Campaign seemed like an eternity, says Norma on the night of victory

JOHN Major has spoken of the path to power from the backstreets of London to Britain's youngest Prime Minister this century.

"It's a long way from Brixton to No 10 Downing Street," he said.

The MP for Huntingdon, brought up in the tough London district, was unruffled after his astonishing victory.

In his first face-to-face interview he said: "I know what lies ahead and I will do it as well as I can." The 47-year-old premier gave the interview just minutes after a congratulatory telephone call from American President George Bush.

Mr Major sent for News reporter Julian Makey and photographer Roger Adams as they waited among the world's press in Downing Street. Then, after hearing Mr Bush's congratulations, Mr Major and his wife Norma chatted freely to the News.

The Prime Minister said he was aware of the task which lay ahead of him in reuniting the party and facing the next General Election.

He was clearly elated by the backing he received from fellow Conservative MPs which left him just two votes short of overall victory in the second ballot.

Then Mr Heseltine and Mr Hurd declared their support for Mr Major, leaving the path to No 10 clear.

Mr Major, who took on the job of running Britain after a meteoric political rise over just 11 years, said today in his first statement as Prime Minister: "I want to see us build a country that is at ease with itself, a country that is confident, and a country that is able and willing to build a better quality of life for all its citizens."

He was speaking outside 10 Downing Street after meeting the Queen to go through the formalities of taking over the reins of Government – with Norma at his side.

Mr Major had said he intended to carry on with his regular visits to his

CAMBRIDGE EVENING NEWS

Huntingdon constituency.

"I shall still be coming home to Huntingdon," he said. Mr Major paid tribute to his campaign team and supporters who had offered a headquarters and staff within hours of his decision to stand.

Mrs Major said that she was "elated" by the result, but that it had still not sunk in.

"I think the team were very confident, but it was difficult to judge from what you were hearing," she said.

"I can't believe it, it is fantastic," she said. "I am looking forward to it." Mrs Major revealed that she had been given a map of her new home at No 10.

"I have got a map, but I haven't had a chance to look at it," she said.

Mrs Major also spoke of the anguish she faced during the election campaign, and was glad that it had finished without going to the third ballot.

"The campaign had gone on long enough," she said. "I know it would only have been another two days, but it seemed like an eternity."

Radio Cambridgeshire also had a world broadcasting exclusive with a telephone interview with Mr Major.

CLASSLESS CANDIDATE WITH GRANDEST AND OLDEST NAME

THE next prime minister has by far the grandest and oldest name of the three candidates. This sits quite oddly on the candidate who claims to be classless and have the common touch, and who is (in spite of propaganda to the contrary) well to the left of his party.

Major is the only leading political name that came over with the Normans.

Major can be a cognate of the Jewish eastern Ashkenazic Mayer.

But as an English name it comes from the Norman personal name Malg(i)er or Maug(i)er, which is composed of the Germanic elements madal, council, plus gari or geri, a spear. The first Majors to come to the top in England were, onomastically, and probably bloodily also, warlords, like the rest of the Norman gangsters.

Mrs Major keeps up the blue-blooded Norman connection by having Norma as her Christian name. In fact, qua Christian name, Norma was invented by Felice Romani in his libretto for Bellini's opera of that name.

The new prime minister's first name was made important and famous by early Christianity. John is the English form of the Latin Johannes, from the New Testament Greek Ioannes. And that is a Greeked and contracted form of the Old Testament Hebrew name Johanan which, being translated, means "God is gracious". The translators of the Authorised Version decided on John as the English way to spell it.

John is the name of several characters in the Old Testament, including one of King David's "mighty men".

The name was borne by John the Baptist (the precursor of Christ himself, who baptised sinners in the River Jordan), by one of Christ's first disciples (John the Apostle, a fisherman, brother of James), and by the author of the fourth gospel (John the Evangelist, identified in Christian tradition with the apostle, but more probably a Greek-speaking Jewish Christian living more than half a century later).

THE TIMES

7

Prime Minister

A breath of fresh air swept through Westminster with the departure of Mrs Thatcher from Number 10. Her autocratic style of conviction politics was to be replaced, the new Prime Minister declared, with a listening Government, one where debate would lead to consensus.

His style quickly became clear in his first Cabinet. The door was re-opened for the return of Michael Heseltine, whose most important task, ironically, was to reform the hated poll tax.

With just a few deft touches, it seemed that a new generation had taken over, and the hand on the tiller was John Major's.

The busy life of a new Prime Minister: testing the produce while visiting a mushroom farm in his constituency, below left; *presenting British Telecom Young Deaf Achievers of the Year awards,* below right; *his first Prime Minister's question time in the House of Commons,* above.

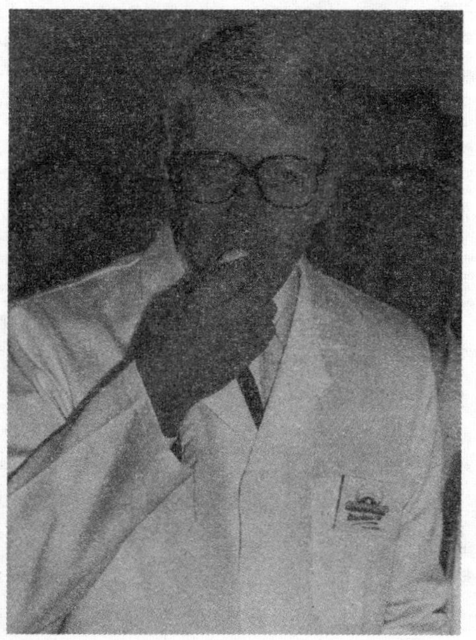

I'm his minder but don't quote me ...

You won't see him quoted on the record again. From today he will be known as 'official sources'.

But last night Downing Street's new press secretary, Gus O'Donnell, spoke to the Daily Mail about his new role as the Government's voice, his relationship with John Major and his rise to the post of Britain's most important 'minder'.

The 38-year-old inheritor of Bernard Ingham's mantle shares more than a passion for football with his boss.

Both are 'grammar school boys made good' who rose to the top through sheer effort and talent rather than rank and privilege.

They are family men who share a vision of a classless Britain. They share a disarmingly dry sense of humour. And both are modest in the extreme about their meteoric rise.

'John Major is such a nice guy that working for him makes

It's not just the ministers and MPs of Government who hold the strings of power in Whitehall and Westminster. There is a whole world behind the scenes, and at the top of that world are the people appointed to the personal staff of the Prime Minister.

Mrs Thatcher's press secretary Bernard Ingham earned himself a degree of notoriety for his blunt and outspoken expressions of her views when he briefed lobby journalists at their daily meetings, but he was undoubtedly a powerful figure in the political hierarchy.

The row over adviser Sir Alan Walters, which led to the resignation of Nigel Lawson, was a clear indication of the importance of the backroom team.

John Major's first appointment was his press secretary, Gus O'Donnell, who was soon followed through the doors of Downing Street by the head of Major's policy unit, economist Sarah Hogg, and political secretary Judith Chaplin. They are key figures in his premiership.

everything worthwhile,' said Mr O'Donnell.

Mr O'Donnell, who was press secretary for former Chancellor Nigel Lawson, first worked with Mr Major when the Premier was Chief Secretary to the Treasury. They hit it off right away and continued working together when Mr Major became Chancellor.

'I'm not one of those people who plan their careers,' he said. 'If there are good opportunities, you take them.' Mr O'Donnell was the youngest of five children raised in a Roman Catholic family between Tooting and Balham in South London, just a few miles from where Mr Major grew up. He attended a Catholic grammar school and went on to study economics at Warwick University.

He married his wife Melanie in 1979. Three weeks ago she gave birth to their first daughter Kirsty Elizabeth.

Mr O'Donnell is a key part of the 'Kitchen Cabinet' that will be installed at Number 10 over the next few weeks.

Another important member of the team will be Mr Major's PPS Graham Bright, 48. His job will be to keep his boss in touch with the mood of the Tory rank and file.

DAILY MAIL

There was deep resentment among the nation's Tory faithful at the apparently abrupt replacement of their idol, Mrs Thatcher, and for some, this led to the start of a campaign for revenge against supporters of Michael Heseltine.

Major pleads for Heseltine backers

By Richard Ford,

Political Correspondent

THE PRIME MINISTER will appeal for party unity next week in an attempt to end conflict in a number of constituencies where supporters of Mr Heseltine face the possibility of being deselected by activists loyal to Mrs Thatcher.

Mr Major's attempt to restore harmony will be made at a meeting in London on Tuesday when he will, under Conservative rules, "be presented for confirmation as party leader".

A senior aide said: "He is not a vengeful person. He will try to get that message across."

Kenneth Baker, the former party chairman and his successor, Chris Patten, have also appealed for peace and harmony, but stressed that they have little power to intervene to halt any moves towards deselecting MPs.

Several prominent backbench supporters of Mr Heseltine are facing difficulties with their local constituency associations for supporting the former defence secretary. Michael Mates, the MP for East Hampshire, faces a resolution calling for the start of a selection procedure to choose a new candidate for his seat on December 17.

In Bexleyheath, the conservative agent has had 500 telephone calls and 200 letters about the leadership. Most oppose the action of the MP Cyril Townsend, who backed Mr Heseltine.

The local association will hold a meeting on January 3 to discuss the leadership election, and Mr Townsend will be asked to explain his actions. "We cannot brush this under the carpet as it would blow up again in six or nine months' time," Mr Alec Mayne, the agent, said.

Yesterday Gerry Neale, a member of Mrs Thatcher's campaign team, was in the Torridge and West Devon constituency where the MP Emma Nicholson has been criticised for switching her support from Mrs Thatcher to Mr Heseltine. Although the constituency agent has received phone calls and letters calling for Miss Nicholson to be deselected, Mr Neale urged reconciliation and unity.

Calls have been made for the resignation of Sir Peter Tapsell, MP for East Lindsey, Lincolnshire, who nominated Mr Heseltine in the leadership contest. Some party members say that his role in Mrs Thatcher's fall from power was unforgivable.

THE TIMES

Chris Patten, appointed Chairman of the Conservative Party by party leader John Major.

John Major's Government appointments were not without a degree of controversy, especially over his Cabinet appointees, who did not include a woman. It was talent for the job, not gender, that determined his selection, it was said. It was also noticed that he had made every effort to heal the wounds of the campaign by making appointments among his rivals' supporters.

Major promotes young blood

By Richard Ford

Political Correspondent

THE PRIME MINISTER last night highlighted his concern for the sporting prowess of the nation's youth by shifting responsibility for sport from the environment to the education department.

John Major also introduced younger blood into the government with the appointment of three back bench MPs, including a woman, to their first ministerial jobs. The changes involved the promotion of two of Douglas Hurd's supporters showing the prime minister's desire for unity. Mr Major is expected to announce further changes to his Government on Monday.

Robert Atkins retains his job as sports minister but responsibility for sport is moved to the education and science department. A Downing Street spokesman said that this reflected Mr Major's interest in sport, particularly among young people.

Tim Yeo, aged 45, parliamentary private secretary to Douglas Hurd, joins the environment department as a parliamentary under secretary. Ann Widdecombe, 43, who supported Mr Hurd in the leadership contest, becomes a parliamentary under secretary in the social security department. Michael Jack, aged 44, joins the social security department as a junior minister.

THE TIMES

First woman 'a bad choice'

Patrick Wintour
Political Correspondent

Ann Widdecombe, the passionate anti-abortionist, yesterday became the first woman to be promoted to government by John Major, as Lynda Chalker, the Overseas Development Minister, deepened Mr Major's embarrassment over his handling of his reshuffle by confirming she had rejected his offer to become the Conservative Party's deputy chairman.

Mrs Chalker had been expecting to be promoted to the Cabinet, which instead is entirely male. Mr Major has come under attack for excluding women from his Cabinet and any kudos in promoting Ms Widdecombe, MP for Maidstone, was lessened in some women's eyes yesterday by her opposition to abortion.

Labour, increasingly optimistic that Mr Major may prove accident prone, also attacked the fact that she had been made a junior minister at the Department of Social Security, claiming that she was likely to use the department as a base from which to try to drive women back into the home. The Labour MP Audrey Wise, a member of the health select committee along with Ms

GUARDIAN

Ann Widdecombe

Widdecombe, said: "This is an extraordinary appointment, particularly in view of her record of opposing an otherwise unanimous select committee report on the need for more careers. Judging by her utterances, she is a member of the diehard 'woman-back-to-the-home league'."

Mr Major, who left Downing Street last night for Cambridgeshire – accompanied by his wife Norma, carrying a teddy bear – has promised to appoint a woman cabinet minister soon.

But Labour leader, Neil Kinnock, dubbing Mr Major "son of handbag", kept up the attack by saying that the new Prime Minister had displayed "prejudice, ignorance and thoughtlessness".

Speaking in Leeds, he said Mr Major had "better wake up to the fact that now in the nineties, it is simply not acceptable for a Prime Minister in a democracy to exclude women from the Cabinet".

Mr Major's embarrassment was deepened by the confirmation from Mrs Chalker that she had turned down the deputy chairman's job after Mr Major told her she was not being promoted to the Cabinet. Mrs Chalker met Mr Major twice this week before rejecting the post.

As the senior woman minister outside the Cabinet, she might have been expected to be angered by Mr Major's explanation that there had been no woman of sufficient merit to be promoted. But Mrs Chalker insisted yesterday that she had not been angry, ending her discussions with Mr Major with a kiss and hug.

She said she was not willing to leave the Overseas Development Administration and felt the job could not be combined with the deputy chairmanship. Mr Major wanted Mrs Chalker to play a key role in the run-up to the election, campaigning in northern marginals.

The Widdecombe appointment demonstrated Mr Major's desire to maintain balance, since Ms Widdecombe played a prominent role in Douglas Hurd's campaign team, as did another new boy to government announced yesterday – Tim Yeo, Mr Hurd's parliamentary private secretary, who is to join the Department of Environment as an under secretary.

Mr Major continued to reward his campaign team when he promoted Michael Jack as a second under secretary at social security.

The previous junior minister at the department, Gillian Shephard, has been appointed the number three at the Treasury. Mr Jack had been PPS to the agriculture minister, John Gummer.

Mr Major also announced that his recently appointed PPS, Graham Bright, would continue in his role.

He switched the minister of sport portfolio from Environment at the same level, while David Heathcoat-Amory, the junior environment minister, takes Mr Baldry's post at the Energy Department.

The Prime Minister enlivens a Christmas party for disabled children.

European issues remained at the forefront of the problems to be faced by the new Government, and the first priority was to ensure that policy was clearly thought through.

Hurd to set out European policy

By Nicholas Wood
Political Correspondent

John Major has acted to end the divisions among his ministers and back benchers that lay behind Margaret Thatcher's downfall.

The prime minister has asked Douglas Hurd, the foreign secretary, to go ahead with a policy paper on Britain's attitude to the European community that will provide a pointer to the government's approach in the sensitive negotiations beginning in Rome in less than two weeks on closer union.

Government sources disclosed that the decision to proceed with the document, first hinted at by Mr Hurd two weeks ago, was taken at Thursday's cabinet. It is assumed in the Foreign Office that the document will be published but that is not confirmed.

Earlier this week, Mr Hurd said he had not been able to win Mrs Thatcher's agreement to publication of what would effectively be a white paper on Europe. All resistance to the document apparently evaporated at the first cabinet presided over by Mr Major.

Ministers discussed the Rome inter-governmental conferences (IGCs) on political and monetary union on Thursday. According to government sources Mr Major then asked Mr Hurd to produce the document.

It is understood that the Foreign Office is trying to meet the December 14 deadline for the opening of the IGCs. However, given the complexity of the issues to be covered and the need to take the paper through the usual policy-making process of cabinet committee, it may not appear until the new year. Foreign Office sources said Mr Hurd would not be stampeded into producing an ill-prepared text.

Labour, which is moving towards acceptance of a single currency, yesterday dismissed the government's move as an exercise in papering over the cracks rather than putting forward genuine policy proposals. Roy Hattersley, the party's deputy leader, said the Tories were still seriously split over Europe.

Conservative Euro-sceptics will be concerned that the Foreign Office has emerged as the leading ministry in drawing up the document, given its traditionally pro-European stance.

The Bruges Group said: "The European issue is not one of style but of substance. It is not a question of how the Prime Minister tackles negotiations on monetary and political union but the result." The statement ended: "Mr Major, we are watching you like a hawk."

However, those Conservatives who want to see Britain adopt a more enthusiastic attitude towards the EC will be encouraged that the foreign secretary's initiative has been given the Prime Minister's blessing.

THE TIMES

The proposed paper is expected to set out the government philosophical stance towards the community, emphasising its belief in a free market, free trading and open and liberal organisation. It would go on to set out policy on a single currency and political union, bringing together positions set out by both Mr Major and Mr Hurd in recent months.

The former chancellor is the author of the "hard ecu" but is opposed to the imposition of a single currency. Mr Hurd has said the EC must clarify the level at which decisions are taken and has declared his opposition to a big extension of qualified majority voting or substantial new powers for the European Parliament. He has backed greater co-ordination of foreign policy and has called for more efficiency and democratic accountability in the community.

Mr Hurd first revealed his interest in the document clarifying the government's stance on November 16 when he said in Leeds that after the leadership contest, the cabinet would have to "draw the threads together" over policy towards the EC.

A visit to a constituency school where, once again, John Major is the target of all the cameras.

It wasn't all an easy ride for the new Prime Minister as he set about his duties...

Souvenir hunter left PM speechless

By Nicholas Wood, Political Correspondent

JOHN MAJOR was temporarily lost for words at his first speaking engagement as prime minister, it was disclosed yesterday.

After his nervous debut as prime minister at the Commons dispatch box on Thursday, he fumbled another chance when he rose to speak to the annual dinner of Altrincham and Sale Conservatives around 10pm that day.

The text of his speech, distributed to political reporters in London more than an hour before, had mysteriously disappeared from the table at which the prime minister was sitting with Sir Fergus Montgomery, the local MP, and Beryl Collins, chairman of the association. Mr Major told the 220 guests at the Cresta Court Hotel, Altrincham, that somebody had apparently walked off with his speech.

"It wasn't a very good speech anyway," he joked. "Never mind, I'll give another one." His audience was not disappointed. The prime minister spoke off-the-cuff and, according to the Tory central office press officer with him, covered the areas set out in his text.

"Only the words were slightly different. The sentiment was the same," his press officer said. The missing text was not found.

Mr Major had been signing programmes and menus for the party faithful before finding himself in the predicament every after-dinner speaker dreads. It is thought that a particularly enthusiastic souvenir hunter was responsible.

Mr Major was fulfilling an engagement made two years ago, when he was chief secretary to the Treasury. He had had to cancel it once because it clashed with the budget.

The prime minister's awkward moment was confirmed by government sources. They said that he frequently ad libbed at such gatherings and that reporters should take care to check his words against a printed text. That would have proved difficult in Altrincham, however, since the press was excluded from the dinner.

"He very rarely sticks to the text. He tends to ad lib. He was forced to ad lib rather more than usual last night," a senior government source said yesterday.

Mr Major's supposed remarks, in which he set out his vision of a softer, more compassionate Conservatism and struck a more positive attitude towards Europe than his predecessor, were widely reported on the front pages of yesterday's newspapers.

Only 220 Tories know whether the papers were telling the whole truth and nothing but the truth.

Mr Major's discomfiture paled into insignificance alongside the indignity once visited on Sir Geoffrey Howe, however, whose Commons speech paved the way for the former chancellor's accession. He once lost his trousers on a train in China.

THE TIMES

... and there was no shortage of advice for Mrs Major as she faced the rigours of life as the Prime Minister's wife.

No 10 hostess is given a few tips by the experts

by Nicholas Watt

NORMA MAJOR will not be short of advice on how to handle the strain of becoming a leading public figure overnight. Although she wants family life to carry on as normal, she will inevitably have to carry out public duties on official occasions.

According to Susan Crosland, the widow of Anthony Crosland, the late foreign secretary, her self esteem and sense of the right priorities will ensure that Mrs Major adapts to the stresses.

In her early public appearances Mrs Major seemed nervous and uncertain. She told interviewers that she felt "physically sick with terror" when her husband became foreign secretary. She has also insisted on maintaining her family life with their two teenage children at their Huntingdon home rather than move to No 10.

Mrs Crosland admires Mrs Major for standing firm: "She does not intend her family life to be locked in the embrace of those civil servants perched in offices all over No 10. And she certainly isn't interested in ad men and fashion writers telling her how she could look 38 if only she took their advice."

Dr Robert Cohen, a consultant psychiatrist at London's Charter Nightingale Hospital, said Mrs Major's insistence on wearing unspectacular clothes and keeping the family together showed she was "tenaciously holding on to" her familiar ways and would undoubtedly be stung by comments about her unimaginative dress sense because "you need the skin of a rhino" to laugh them off. As an intelligent person she would cope with the changes imposed on her life if she tackled them gradually. She would, however, experience enormous anxiety as she tried to adapt.

Another London doctor said that Mrs Major could, at first, feel very insecure at official functions and that her hosts should integrate her into the gathering.

Norma Major, now also a focus of media attention.

Reform of the poll tax was one of Major's key election pledges.

BREAK
THE TORY
POLL TAX
PAY
NO
POLL
TAX
BREAK
THE TORY
POLL TAX
DON'T PAY
DON'T COLLECT
DON'T
PAY

Major sets out radical agenda for social unity

By Julia Langdon and David Wastell

MR MAJOR has convinced the Cabinet that the Conservatives can win the next General Election if Government policy reflects his own agenda for a radical programme designed to promote social unity.

In the aftermath of the damaging leadership election, the new Prime Minister wants to build on his success of reuniting the Conservative party by demonstrating his concern for greater social cohesion.

He wants his new Cabinet to put more emphasis on policies for the inner cities, to provide help for the family and to end the North-South divide in addition to reforming the poll tax in a politically viable and publicly acceptable way. He is also expected to order an urgent review of child benefit. In his first week at Number 10, Mr Major has concentrated on securing a Government which will demonstrate his concensual approach, without offending former supporters of Mrs Thatcher. He is said to be enormously encouraged by the response from the Conservative party, but wants to unite the country as well as his own supporters. He will make a public appeal for clemency within the Conservative party when he is officially acclaimed as leader at a formal meeting of MPs, peers and the National Union

SUNDAY TELEGRAPH

at Central Hall, Westminster, on Tuesday.

While there is continuing disquiet among party activists about the treatment of Mrs Thatcher, her successor wants to ensure there are no further recriminations against MPs by their local members for alleged disloyalty.

Mr Major is already committed to fundamental changes in the poll tax through the appointment of Michael Heseltine as Secretary of State for the Environment. Mr Heseltine will disclose his approach in the House of Commons this week in a debate instigated by Labour on Wednesday.

While the options are limited and the timetable restricted by the need to move before this year's community charge levels are set, Mr Heseltine has been given a free rein. "It would be ridiculous for the Prime Minister to appoint him then insist on him producing a mouse," one Whitehall source said.

Although Mr Major suffered a slight setback by not appointing a woman to his first Cabinet, he could make good his omission with his approach to child benefit.

The signs are that he will order a rethink on child benefit which, until the £1 concession for first children in the Autumn statement, had remained frozen for three years. This could produce a move towards re-establishing the link with the inflation rate and may also lead to changes in the tax system.

One suggestion under consideration is to increase the benefit substantially but count it as taxable income for working mothers.

Considerable attention was also being paid yesterday to Mr Major's first speech as Prime Minister in Manchester when he said: "There is life north of Watford – lots of it," and promised that a better future based on new industries, enterprises and investments was now possible.

"I think it was inevitable that once Mrs Thatcher had gone, the party would move in this direction," one Minister said yesterday. "There was no credible way of leading much further down the Thatcherite road." Mr Major passed his first electoral test with last week's Scottish by-elections in Paisley in which the Tories fared rather better than they might have expected under Mrs Thatcher. His next test will be a by-election in the Ribble Valley, the constituency of Mr David Waddington who takes his seat in the Lords on Tuesday.

John Major's successor as Chancellor of the Exchequer, Norman Lamont, a leading member of the Major campaign team.

After Mrs Thatcher's defeat in the leadership election, there was a great danger that the Thatcherite wing of the Tory Party would seek revenge on those seen as responsible for her downfall. It was vital that John Major unite the party as quickly as possible without losing sight of his own objectives and policies.

Tories hear new call to unity

By ROBIN OAKLEY, Political Editor

IN HIS first address to the party faithful yesterday Mr Major set out a political credo, offering his party flexible, commonsense Conservatism which was willing to adjust policies which did not work.

The prime minister emphasised the importance of compassion and used notably more moderate language about Europe than Margaret Thatcher, to whom he paid lavish tribute. He also threw his weight behind John Taylor, the black prospective candidate whose selection for Cheltenham has provoked a racist backlash. Mr Major said: 'We believe that every man and woman should be able to go as far as their talent, ambition and effort take them. There should be no artificial barrier of background, religion or race.'

He warned Conservatives that without unity they would never achieve the success they had achieved under Mrs Thatcher, and in a clear signal to constituency associations to call off any action planned against MPs who supported Michael Heseltine in the leadership battle, he urged his party to reject back-biting, recriminations and inquests, saying: 'There is too much at stake. We have an election to win.'

Setting out his beliefs, Mr Major put first the need for the conquest of inflation, calling it 'economically destructive and socially divisive' and urged the need for savings. Signalling his government's willingness to be adaptable, he said: 'Where we find that things are not quite right, we will listen, and we will make the changes that are necessary. That is precisely why we have put in hand a further review of the community charge.' On Europe, Mr Major said that Britain had to be 'in there arguing, persuading and, yes, fighting for our interests'.

THE TIMES

In the early days of his political career, John Major at a Young Conservatives function.

Tory leaders move swiftly to back black candidate

Black barrister John Taylor's selection to fight the Cheltenham seat for the Conservatives prompted a serious and widely reported row in the constituency party, with many members seeking to put forward a local candidate. But the Tory leadership, headed by John Major, threw its weight behind Mr Taylor.

by Philip Webster, Chief Political Correspondent

John Major and other senior Conservatives acted last night to quell a damaging race dispute by disowning protests by party activists over the choice of a black Tory parliamentary candidate.

The prime minister and Chris Patten, the Tory chairman, swung the full weight of the party machine behind John Taylor, who has been selected as the prospective candidate for Cheltenham in the face of some local opposition.

Mr Major said: "As long as I am privileged to lead our party it will never become an exclusive club." Racist remarks aimed at the man who is tipped to be the first black Tory MP were "not sentiments that have any place in our party".

Last night, in a letter to Roy Hattersley, deputy leader of the Labour party, Mr Major said: "I will have no truck with racism. As I said this morning, my hope is to build a truly open society in which every man and woman should be able to go as far as their talent, ambition and effort take them. There should be no artificial barrier of background, race or religion. This should be the essence of Conservatism."

There is anger and embarrassment among Tory MPs and at Conservative Central Office at the outburst from Bill Galbraith, a local party member, who was reported as calling Mr Taylor, a former adviser to the Home Office, a "bloody nigger".

Mr Galbraith, who tried to black Mr Taylor's adoption, was reported as saying the people of Cheltenham wanted a local man and not "a nigger from Birmingham". Although Mr Galbraith, a cousin of the Earl of Strathclyde, said yesterday the remarks were made in private and that he had been misquoted, he admitted: "I did say that we would not let bloody niggers into this town."

Last night Roy Hattersley, Labour's deputy leader, urged Mr Major to expel Mr Galbraith.

Mr Patten wrote congratulating Mr Taylor on his selection as candidate and wishing him every success. "I know how much work you have done for the party over many years and I well understand why your qualities commended themselves to the Cheltenham association," he said.

Mr Patten told BBC Radio 4's The World at One that Mr Taylor was selected on merit. "I do not think that anybody has any time at all for the rather repellent views of a minority in our society." Asked if there were constituencies where racist views were widely represented, Mr Patten replied: "There are people embracing every political creed who have views on race that make Alf Garnett seem like a screaming liberal."

Mr Taylor again brushed aside the candidacy dispute. "I am not worried about that, I have a job to do, it is a very enjoyable job and that is getting to know the people of Cheltenham." He said there was "no question" about the support of the Cheltenham Tory association, which had selected him from 250 hopefuls. Mr Taylor later added: "You will always get people in society whose vision does not extend beyond the end of their noses. Frankly I feel sorry for people like that."

Meanwhile, the Commission for Racial Equality received calls yesterday from people complaining about Mr Galbraith's comments. The Freedom Association urged the Director for Public Prosecutions to prosecute him under the Public Order Act.

THE TIMES

NEW PREMIER IS A MAJOR BOOST FOR YARWOOD

By LOUISE GAHHON

He made his name as Harold Wilson. And now he's making a comeback – as John Major.

This is the impression which looks set to revive Mike's career. The star's amazing likeness to the new Prime Minister was unveiled on last night's Des O'Connor Tonight programme on ITV. Yarwood's career declined after Mrs Thatcher became Premier years ago. But he hopes his Major mimic will help put him back on top.

"There is still more work to be done on it but I was delighted to give my Mr Major his first airing," he said.

"With all my previous Prime Ministers, I had to be aged with make-up. But Mr Major is actually slightly younger than me so it makes a nice change."

The 1980s were an unhappy time for 49-year-old Yarwood as he found himself overshadowed by stars like Faith Brown and Bobby Davro. Thames TV refused to renew his £250,000 a year contract, claiming his jokes were too old-fashioned. Yarwood's personal life was even more traumatic. His 18-year marriage ended in 1985 and a year later he received a three-year ban for drink driving.

As his health deteriorated, he collapsed on stage three times and was forced to withdraw from a pantomime.

Yarwood: "I suffered a heart attack in July this year." But a spokesman for the star said last night: "He has now fully recovered and is really raring to go. He's back with a vengeance. There's been an enormous amount of interest in Mike since the arrival of Mr Major."

DAILY MAIL

Norma Major in sunny mood

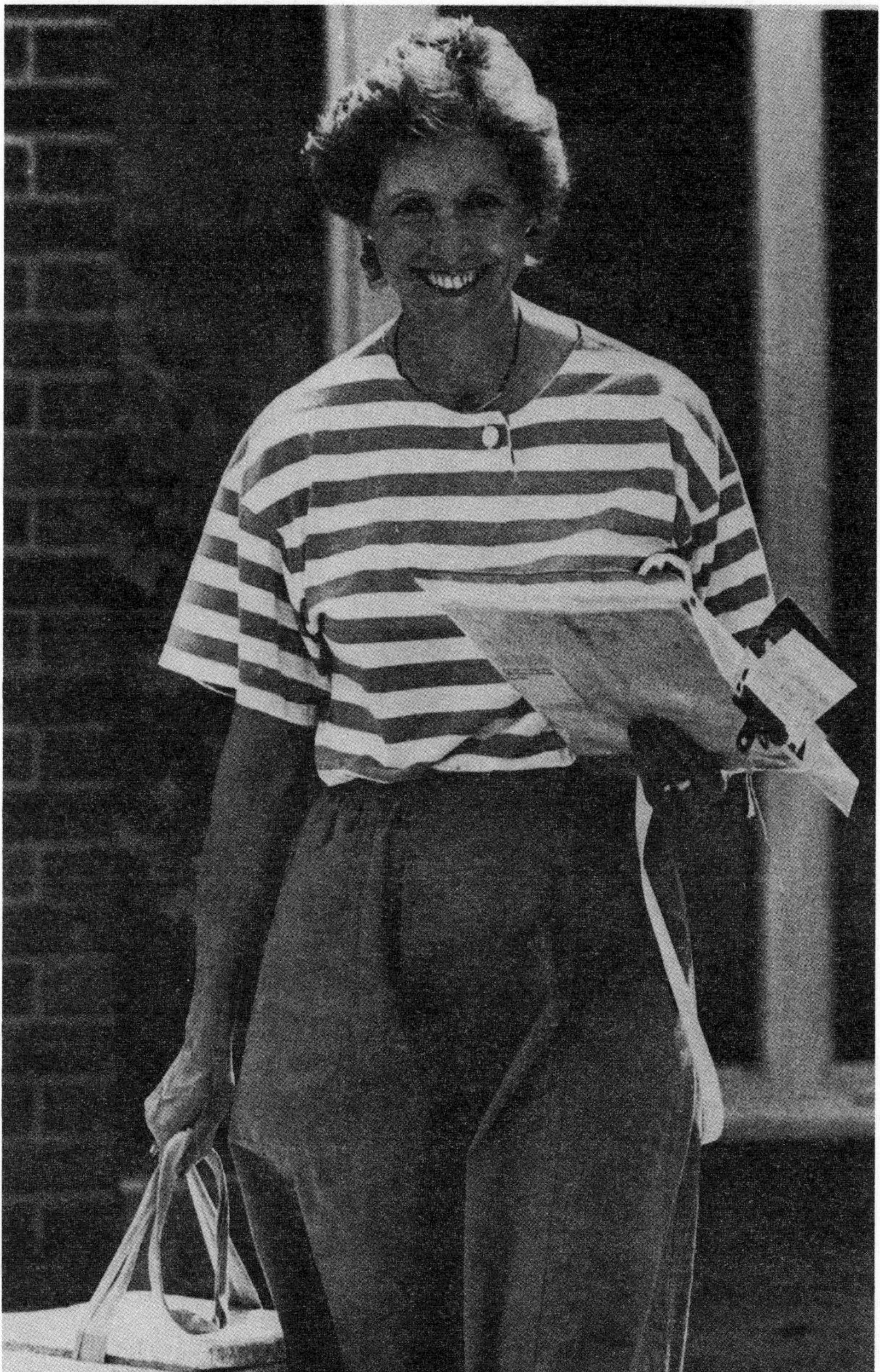

Policy chief's political pedigree

By MICHAEL TREND

MRS SARAH HOGG, Economics Editor of The Daily Telegraph and wife of Mr Douglas Hogg, Foreign Office Minister, was appointed director of the Central Policy Unit at 10 Downing Street yesterday. This represents one of the most important staff appointments made by Mr Major since he became Prime Minister.

Mrs Hogg developed a warm working relationship with Mr Major first when he was Chief Secretary at the Treasury and then when he was Chancellor. Aged 44, she is widely recognised as one of the ablest and most imaginative of her generation, and established a formidable reputation as City Editor of the Independent, and subsequently at The Daily Telegraph.

Her political pedigree will stand her in good stead in her new position: her father, Lord Boyd-Carpenter, was Chief Secretary to the Treasury under Harold Macmillan and Sir Alec Douglas-Home. She married a childhood friend, the son of the former Lord Chancellor, Lord Hailsham; they have two children, a daughter and a son. Born to politics, Mrs Hogg has had an outstanding career in journalism, working for the Economist, The Sunday Times, The Times and Channel 4 News before joining the newly-founded Independent to set up its business and finance pages.

But readers of The Daily Telegraph have seen her full talents at their best.

In what Mrs Hogg described yesterday as a 'wonderfully happy year', she wrote a weekly economics column, which appeared on the centre pages of this newspaper.

It was quickly recognised as peerless in its field. With an elegance of style and a welcoming approach she won readers who, in other circumstances, would have passed over any economics article with a groan or a shudder. In her articles she combined a profound grasp of economic issues with a rigorous appreciation of the political art of the possible.

Mr Max Hastings, Editor-in-Chief of The Daily Telegraph, said yesterday: 'We are all very saddened to lose such an outstanding journalist from our own staff but we could not be more delighted for Sarah. Her energy and extraordinary clarity of thought will be tremendous assets to the Policy Unit.'

DAILY TELEGRAPH

Mrs Hogg was offered her new position on Tuesday night. Having joined her husband to greet the President of the Gambia at the Phoenix Theatre, she slipped away to Downing Street, missing the first act of Stephen Sondheim's Into the Woods. She returned for the interval to tell her husband that she would shortly be joining him in the corridors of power.

Yesterday Mrs Hogg said that she was 'absolutely delighted with my new appointment. I cannot think of anyone that I would rather do this job for.' But she also bade farewell – for the moment, at least – to her large following among newspaper readers by adding that 'from now on, I fear, my opinions are for internal consumption only'.

TOP NO 10 JOB GOES TO WOMAN

By ROBERT MORGAN

ANOTHER WOMAN has been appointed to a top position in the government. Downing Street announced last night that the prime minister had appointed Judith Chaplin to be his political secretary and head of his political office. Mrs Chaplin was John Major's special adviser when he was Chancellor of the Exchequer.

Last week, Mr Major appointed head of the Downing Street policy unit Sarah Hogg, a financial journalist and wife of the foreign office minister Douglas Hogg.

The task of the political office is to provide the link between the prime minister and the Conservative party and to give advice and support on political engagements and speeches. The office is situated in No 10 but financed by the party. Mrs Chaplin worked for the Conservative research department in London before becoming head of the policy unit at the Institute of Directors.

In October 1988, Nigel Lawson, then Chancellor, made her his special adviser.

So you think you want to be Prime Minister. Here's the book that tells you how.

Major pledges another £42m for haemophiliacs

By ROBIN OAKLEY and JILL SHERMAN

The prime minister yesterday bowed to political and public pressure and agreed to pay a further £42 million to haemophiliacs infected with the Aids virus through contaminated health service blood products.

The Haemophilia Society said the money, an average £35,000 for each of the 1,200 victims or their families, was 'a triumph for a caring government under John Major, but a tragedy for the haemophiliacs' campaign'. The Society, which had been hoping for £90 million, argued that the sum was too little, too late and that it failed to provide adequate compensation for those infected. Two hundred and sixteen have developed Aids and 150 have died.

The handout represents a reversal of government policy. Margaret Thatcher and Kenneth Clarke, the former health secretary, had insisted that the matter should be settled by the courts. But yesterday, William Waldegrave, the health secretary, who had discussed the issue with Mr Major and the new Chief Secretary to the Treasury, David Mellor, said: 'A number of fresh minds came to look at this.' The prime minister underlined that the Conservative party was under new management by announcing the concession himself during Commons question time. The government had accepted an offer from the lawyers representing the haemophiliacs, he said.

Mr Waldegrave said later that the £42 million would be in addition to the £34 million already allocated. The money would be distributed by the MacFarlane Trust and be exempt from social security clawbacks, saving the average family of two £10,000. The government would also meet all 'reasonable' legal costs, expected to amount to around £2 million.

However, the health department made clear that the offer was conditional on all the litigants dropping their cases. Ministers also insisted that it was a final offer, not the opening of a bargaining process.

The cases were brought earlier this year after more than four years' campaigning by haemophiliacs and their families. The plaintiffs argued that the government's failure to ensure that England and Wales were self-sufficient in blood products led to most of the victims being infected by contaminated blood products from America before 1985.

Mr Waldegrave said the government had considered proposals from the steering committee of solicitors representing the plaintiffs and agreed that they would provide a fair way of ending the litigation. 'We believe that our case is legally strong and that the plaintiffs would not succeed in proving negligence on the part of the Department of Health,' he said.

'Nevertheless, the government has always recognised the very special and tragic circumstances of the haemophiliacs infected by HIV and their families. We recognise, too, the harrowing effect legal action would have on them.' David Watters, general

THE TIMES

secretary of the Haemophilia Society, expressed grave disappointment at the size of the award. 'John Major and William Waldegrave are to be applauded for addressing the problem so promptly. It is unfortunate the settlement has been so low,' he said.

The solicitors' committee suggested the deal after predicting in September that they might win £90 million in court. The committee said the new figures 'reflect the risk of litigation and the legal hurdles which the plaintiffs must surmount in their litigation against the government and the low level of damages prevailing for personal injuries. The figures do not represent proper compensation in moral terms for this appalling tragedy. That is not their purpose.' The committee had suggested that the government could offer another £20 million.

Besides the £42 million offered yesterday, the government will settle out of court cases where negligence might have been proved, likely to number fifteen. When legal costs are included, the package will be worth between £47 million and £51 million.

Robin Cook, the shadow health secretary, said at Westminster: 'I welcome today's progress. I do hope we are now coming to a solution on this very serious matter. I am glad the government has come down on the side of compassion and commonsense. However, I very much hope that the business will not be buried without getting a proper system of no-fault compensation in place.'

CHAMELEON MAN

John Major's announcement of compensation for haemophiliacs infected with the Aids virus is not the first time he has stolen the Opposition's clothes in such fashion. During the blizzards of January 1987, as social security minister, he announced the government's U-turn on cold-weather payments for the old and infirm. At this signal, of course, temperatures shot up, and an unattributable Treasury source, peeved at the additional £15 million cost, accused the future Chancellor of "handing out warm-weather payments".

When Major became chief secretary to the Treasury he soon clawed the money back. Former colleagues at the DSS expected a sympathetic hearing, but found him more stony-hearted than to any other department.

As Nick Scott, Major's successor, pleaded for urgent extra cash, he was halted in mid-sentence. "It's no good," Major told him. The department had "grossly overspent" its budget for the previous year. Cuts were called for, not extra cash.

Aghast, Scott pointed out that Major, as social security minister, had been the man responsible for the overspend. That was last year, Major replied, and this year he held the purse strings.

THE TIMES

DELORS MAKES 'CRISIS' THREAT TO MAJOR OVER MONETARY UNION

By CHRIS MONCRIEFF and GEOFF MEADE, in ROME

EC Commission president Jacques Delors took the shine off John Major's summit success today, December 15, by warning him against any attempt to derail plans for a single currency and central European bank.

His outburst shattered the end of Mr Major's first EC summit as Prime Minister – a meeting which until then had been hailed as a personal diplomatic triumph.

Mr Delors dropped his bombshell as Mr Major flew back to London from the two-day Rome meeting "very satisfied" at the UK's enhanced Community relations.

The clear implication was that Mr Delors had toppled Mrs Thatcher over the single currency – and the Commission president bluntly warned Mr Major that he could suffer the same fate.

Before the fall, Mrs Thatcher sits grim-faced as her Chancellor speaks in the House of Commons.

"If we need to provoke another political crisis we will do so," Mr Delors said.

Foreign Secretary Douglas Hurd immediately attempted to avert what could be another damaging European confrontation for Britain.

He insisted there had been no crisis at the summit and pleaded: "Don't let's manufacture a crisis."

Mr Delors' remark followed Mr Major's confirmation at the summit that the British Treasury has prepared its own "treaty" on economic and monetary union.

He said it reinforced the Government's "hard Ecu" alternative to the Delors proposal for a one-currency Europe.

However, Mr Delors made it clear months ago he saw the plan as an unneccessary distraction and his remarks today in Rome were the strongest yet.

"I am distrustful and have good reason to be so," he told a news conference as the summit ended.

The Commission president said he had welcomed Mr Major's proposals – made when the Prime Minister was the Chancellor – as a contribution to the single-currency debate.

If Britain accepted a single currency and the central bank, the Community could work together as Twelve. The rest, said Mr Delors, was open for discussion.

"Otherwise we will have a difficult transition to the final phase. Ideas for the use of the Ecu could be incorporated into our project, but to set us off and derail us would be simply a distraction."

Then he threw down the gauntlet to Mr Major, threatening, if necessary, another political crisis.

Mr Major and Mr Delors now find themselves at odds as the inter-governmental conference on economic and monetary union gets under way.

Chancellor Norman Lamont is in the hot seat, promoting Mr Major's own plan in the face of determined opposition from the Commission president.

The British Government believes the Ecu should operate alongside existing national currencies as a common currency and only become a single currency, replacing all others in Europe, if the public chooses.

A single currency by imposition, the Government has insisted, is not acceptable.

Similar strident tones on economic policy triggered Mrs Thatcher's political downfall, for which Mr Delors is now claiming credit.

Later, Mr Hurd told reporters: "It is now time to get down to serious work. To be successful there has to be agreement. As the Prime Minister said, there is no reason why there should not be agreement.

"Don't let's manufacture a crisis. There has been no crisis at this summit.

"Our proposals are about to be put into treaty form. I do not think there is any need for discussions in government in the next few weeks."

Mr Hurd said Britain would promote her own ideas as Mr Delors would promote his.

Earlier, Mr Major had emerged apparently triumphant from the summit, claiming he had succeeded in putting Britain's "favourite dishes" on the menu.

But he warned, too, that he would not hesitate to order the use of the veto if policies emerged from later inter-governmental conferences to which Britain had objections.

THE TIMES

The Prime Minister, relaxed, smiling and jovial, told a crowded news conference he was "very satisfied" with the outcome of the final communique.

He firmly and fiercely rejected the idea that Britain was isolated on the single-currency issue. "Nor do I think we stand alone, as is supposed, on many other issues," he added.

The issues on which Mr Major claimed success for Britain include:

Political union;

Closer co-operation on foreign and security policies;

Food aid and technical assistance to the Soviet Union and Eastern European countries;

A "positive statement" on the international trade crisis;

Renewed support for the UN resolutions on the Gulf crisis;

The immediate ending of sanctions banning investment in South Africa.

The outcome – marred by Mr Delors' outburst – looked like a feather in Mr Major's cap.

He will still win a huge welcome when he makes his Commons statement on the summit on Tuesday and his performance will add to his authority when he meets President Bush at Camp David next week.

The two conferences adjourned in Rome tonight, signalling the start of months of discussions among the EC ministers, diplomats and experts on the future shape of Europe.

Mr Lamont took part in a one-hour meeting with his EC counterparts on plans for a single currency, while Mr Hurd met fellow foreign ministers to start the debate on political union.

Both sessions were largely devoted to organising a hectic schedule of negotiations, ultimately leading to agreements on new EC treaties on economic policy and political union.

Mr Lamont said he had reminded his colleagues of Britain's reluctance to endorse a single currency, pressing instead the case for the "hard Ecu" alternative launched by Mr Major when he was Chancellor.

It was a "very good meeting with a lot of goodwill", said Mr Lamont.

But difficult talks are in prospect, with the Government detemined to push for the Ecu as a common currency, rather than a single currency.

On political union, attention will focus on the amount of legislative powers to be passed to the European Parliament and the complex question of a defence and foreign policy for the EC.

EC leaders had been friendly to Mr Major because of a change in style from Mrs Thatcher's approach, Liberal Democrat Treasury spokesman Alan Beith said tonight.

"The other leaders are so relieved by the welcome change of style and the end of handbag politics that they are ready to give Britain's new Prime Minister the friendly signals and a little more time to get his act together."

CHRONOLOGY

John Roy Major was born on March 29, 1943 in Merton, Surrey. His father, Abraham Thomas Ball, alias Tom Major of the circus double-act Drum and Major, was in his mid-sixties. His mother, Gwen, was 44.

John was the youngest of four children. The eldest, Frank, died in childhood. John's first 10 years were spent in suburban Worcester Park while Tom ran a garden gnome business. But in 1953 the family was forced to move to a two-room flat on Coldharbour Lane, Brixton, after one of Tom's investments went badly wrong.

John Major did not like school. He left Rutlish Grammar School, Wimbledon, at the age of 16, and soon started work as a labourer. He joined the Brixton Young Conservatives in 1960, becoming chairman within a year.

John Major's fortunes began to flourish during the 1960s: after nine months' unemployment he found a career in banking, joining Standard Chartered in 1965. He almost lost his left leg in a car crash while working in Nigeria during the Biafran war.

He also established himself in local politics, founding the Lambeth Borough Young Conservatives in 1965 and, three years later, becoming Lambeth Borough Councillor for the Ferndale ward. His chairmanship of the Housing Committee in 1970-71 won plaudits from a young political rival, Labour left-winger Ken Livingstone.

John Major met Norma Christina Johnson, a domestic science teacher, during the Greater London Council elections in 1970. They married within three months at the church opposite Lambeth Town Hall and have two children, Elizabeth, now 19, and James, 15.

Thereafter, politics took over and John Major's progress up the slippery pole was first steady, then rapid.

1972

January: Major is adopted as prospective parliamentary candidate for Camden, St Pancras North. He claims specialist knowledge of housing, finance, local government and African affairs.

1974

February 28: Prime Minister Edward Heath loses a snap general election while Major finishes second to Labour's Jock Stallard in the St Pancras constituency. He wins 7,926 votes to Mr Stallard's 14,761.

October 10: Labour slightly increases its House of Commons majority under Prime Minister Harold Wilson. Major loses again to Mr Stallard, his share of the vote slipping by 1%.

1976

November 21: Major is chosen to fight the safe seat of Huntingdonshire after Sir David Renton MP announces his intention not to stand again at the next election.

1977

May 6: Major is elected to the GLC. He wins Hornchurch from Labour with a majority of almost 4,000 votes.

1979

May 3: Mrs Thatcher sweeps to power on a tide of Conservative support. Major reaches first base and becomes an MP after romping home in Huntingdonshire. He wins 40,193 votes, increasing the majority by 12,319 to 21,563.

1981

January 26: A first promotion for Major. He is made parliamentary private secretary to Home Office ministers Timothy Raison and Patrick Mayhew.

1983

January 14: Another promotion. Major becomes a junior Government Whip, drawing a salary of £13,275.

June 9: A Conservative landslide majority at the general election gives Mrs Thatcher's Government a second term. Major wins easily in the redrawn seat of Huntingdon with a 20,348 majority, his share of the vote up 7% on 1979.

1984

October 3: Major is made a senior in the Whips' office, a position away from the glare of publicity but regarded as a fast track to the Cabinet.

1985

September 2: A Cabinet reshuffle after the resignation of Environment Secretary Patrick Jenkin brings changes in the Government lower ranks. Major gets his first departmental post as a junior minister at the Department of Health and Social Security.

1986

September 10: Major is promoted to the politically sensitive post of Minister of Social Security in an extensive reshuffle of Government middle ranks. He commands one of the largest budgets in Whitehall.

1987

January 13: Major briefly becomes Public Enemy Number One as he defends tight Government restrictions on cold-weather payments to the old, eventually backing down as sub-zero temperatures plague the country.

June 11: Mrs Thatcher wins another huge majority on a slightly reduced share of the vote. Major further pushes up his Huntingdon vote to make it the safest Conservative seat in the country with a 27,044 majority.

June 1: Major is the first of the class of 1979 MPs to enter the Cabinet. He becomes Chief Secretary to the Treasury, an unpopular post with a simple brief to curb public spending.

October 4: Norman Tebbit becomes the first political heavyweight to tip John Major as a future Tory leader.

1988

October: For the second year running, Major succeeds in resolving the Government public spending round without recourse to the "Star Chamber".

1989

July 24: Major hits the big time, replacing Sir Geoffrey Howe as Foreign Secretary. *The Times* says his rapid advancement as one of Mrs Thatcher's most trusted lieutenants is to counterbalance the promotion of two former wets, as Chris Patten becomes Environment Secretary and Kenneth Baker is made Conservative Party chairman.

October 22: A row over sanctions against South Africa tests Major's mettle as the Commonwealth conference in Kuala Lumpur ends in acrimony. Number 10 aides deny a policy rift with the Prime Minister.

October 26: Nigel Lawson shocks Westminster by resigning as Chancellor of the Exchequer. He blames Mrs Thatcher's political adviser Sir Alan Walters.Major is immediately made the new Chancellor. "It's a job he has always wanted, so I suppose it's good news. But I think it's terrible for Nigel," says Norma.

1990

March 20: Major's first budget is also the first to be televised. His attempt to revive the culture of thrift is well-received by Tory back-benchers, but fails to reassure the City. The pound dips against the D-mark and the dollar as concern over inflation mounts.

March 25: In a Mori/*Sunday Times* opinion poll, just 3% of those questioned back Major to lead the Conservatives into an election; he trails Michael Heseltine (39%), Mrs Thatcher (13%) and Sir Geoffrey Howe (5%).

June 20: Major launches an innovative plan for the so-called hard Ecu in a bid to slow progress towards European Monetary Union while not looking anti-European.

October 5: Major springs a coup on Parliament and the City by announcing Britain's entry into Europe's Exchange Rate Mechanism after years of delay and bitter argument. Interest rates are cut by one point to 14%.

October 9: A Gallup survey finds that 47% of the public recognise John Major's photograph, up from 15% a year before when he was newly-appointed Foreign Secretary.

November 1: Sir Geoffrey Howe resigns. Twelve days later he triggers the leadership battle between Mrs Thatcher and former Defence Secretary Michael Heseltine after a devastating resignation speech in the Commons.

November 22: Margaret Thatcher, with tears in her eyes, tells the Cabinet she will resign. Major and Foreign Secretary Douglas Hurd stand against Heseltine. Before the day is out Major campaigners claim the support of a third of Tory MPs after canvassing barely 70%.

November 27: Major falls two votes short of outright victory in the leadership second ballot. But, minutes later, Heseltine and Hurd throw in the towel.

November 28: Major kisses hands with the Queen at Buckingham Palace to become the youngest PM this century.